THE BIBLE IN 52 WEEKS™ FOR BLACK WOMEN

the BIBLE IN 52 WEEKS™ FOR BLACK WOMEN

A YEARLONG BIBLE STUDY

REV. COURTNEY CLAYTON JENKINS

callisto publishing
an imprint of Sourcebooks

Callisto Publishing LLC

Published by Callisto Publishing LLC C/O Sourcebooks LLC
P.O. Box 4410, Naperville, Illinois 60567-4410
(630) 961-3900
callistopublishing.com

Text by Rev. Courtney Jenkins
Illustrations by Agnieszka Żylińska-Rękas
Author photo courtesy of Natasha Herbert

Series Designer: Liz Cosgrove
Art Director: Lisa Schreiber
Art Producer: Stacey Stambaugh
Editor: Adrian Potts
Production Editor: Rachel Taenzler
Production Designer: Jeffrey Piekarz

Library of Congress Cataloging-in-Publication Data
Names: Jenkins, Courtney Clayton author
Title: The Bible in 52 weeks for Black women : a yearlong Bible study for women / Courtney Clayton Jenkins.
Description: Naperville, Illinois : Callisto Publishing LLC, [2026] | Includes biographical information. | Includes bibliographical references.
Identifiers: LCCN 2025052762 (trade paperback) | LCCN 2025052763 (epub)
Subjects: LCSH: Devotional calendars | Bible—Study and teaching | LCGFT: Meditations
Classification: LCC BV4811 .J38 2026 (print) | LCC BV4811 (ebook)
LC record available at https://lccn.loc.gov/2025052762
LC ebook record available at https://lccn.loc.gov/2025052763

Printed and bound in China
OGP 10 9 8 7 6 5 4 3 2 1

From the seeds planted by my
praying grandmother, to the safety
of my sistah-friends circle, to the
sacred fire inside of every woman
who picks up this offering—
may this book kindle your soul.

CONTENTS

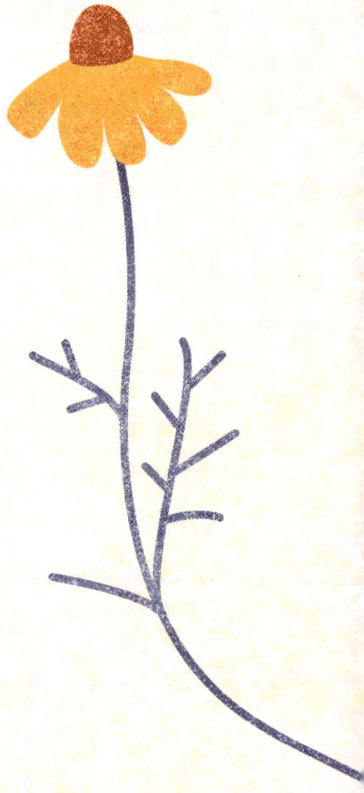

INTRODUCTION

IT WAS MY SENIOR YEAR AT SPELMAN COLLEGE. A photographer had been hired by the college to take our senior portraits. Somehow, a disagreement about Scripture surfaced as I shared my calling to ministry. I can't recall the exact passage we debated, but I'll never forget her repeated response: "Well, my pastor said..." After she gave the same answer nearly a dozen times, I finally paused and asked, "But what have you studied for yourself? What do you say about the Word of God?" She had no clue what the Bible said beyond what her pastor had told her.

If you've picked up this book, chances are you've asked yourself the same thing. The 52 weeks of devotional commentary in this Bible study are for my sistah who is not afraid to wonder. For the one ready to read the Bible with open eyes, deep questions, and sacred curiosity. For the Black woman who dares to believe that Scripture has something to say not just about her—but to her.

I took my own advice to search Scripture for myself and matriculated through Princeton Theological Seminary, where I earned a Master of Divinity. Since 2010, I have served as the senior pastor and teacher of South Euclid United Church of Christ in Cleveland, Ohio. Over and over, I hear a holy hunger for Bible studies that don't just tell us what to think, but also invite us to wrestle with the text.

This book also exists for the woman who's asking, "What am I supposed to do with this?" In a world heavy with injustice, pressure, and performance, we need more than biblical knowledge—we need wisdom that works. Each week, I try to sit with you, page by page, and talk it through. May these pages become your commentary and your divine connection point. A place to ask your questions. A place to belong. A place that feels like home.

SISTERS IN CHRIST

When I think back to that moment in college—the photographer who kept saying, "My pastor said"—I can't help but hear echoes of something from our past. During slavery, when most Black people were forbidden or unable to read, the preacher often had the rare ability to do so. The Word was passed down orally—memorized, repeated, embodied. And that oral tradition still lives on. We hear Scripture in sermons, live streams, smartphone notifications, group texts, and reels sent by friends. We still gather around the Word, even if it's now through apps and earbuds.

However, there comes a moment when you have to ask: *What does this mean for me, personally?*

This devotional commentary is an invitation to that moment in your journey as a Black woman. That's why this book is rooted in a womanist lens—a framework for looking at the Bible that centers the lived experience, spiritual wisdom, and moral agency of Black women. As a womanist preacher, I approach the Bible with deep reverence, and with deep questions. I believe we can worship with awe and wrestle with love. We can sit at the feet of Jesus and reflect on why so few women are named in the Bible, even as they play crucial roles.

Sistahs, it's time to tend to our own vineyards (I'll explain more in week 32). Time to stop living off secondhand faith. Time to study for ourselves. Time to claim the Bible as a mirror, a meal, and a means of liberation.

We've always been in the story. Now let's read the story like we believe it.

HOW TO USE THIS BOOK

The goal of this book is simple, yet sacred: to help you read the entire Bible in one year and grow closer to God, to yourself, and to the abundant life made possible by saying yes to Jesus Christ (John 10:7-10).

I often share my personal motto with my congregation: *Nothing compares to a long walk with God*. That's what this journey will be—a sacred, steady walk. And the Bible? It's our roadmap. Holy. Breathable. Still trustworthy today.

Whether you're reading Scripture for the first time or returning with fresh questions, this book is designed to guide, support, and walk with you. I know the Bible can sometimes feel hard to read—the language unfamiliar, the meaning not always clear. That's why these pages are written to help you not only read the Word, but also understand and apply it to your daily life. You don't have to do it alone. And you don't have to know it all to begin.

WHAT IS THE BIBLE?

The Bible is our roadmap for the long walk with God—66 books written across centuries, cultures, and covenants. It's divided into the Old Testament (39 books) and the New Testament (27 books), and together they reveal the character of a God who loves, creates, liberates, forgives, redeems, restores—and still walks with us every step of the way.

Throughout this book, I'll refer to the New International Version (NIV) for Scripture, but feel free to use whatever version helps you stay consistent and connected. That might be a printed Bible, a phone app, or an audio version you listen to on your commute. The best translation is the one you'll understand.

This book has nothing to do with church, denomination, or preference. It's not about dogma—it's about devotion. It's not about religious performance—it's about spiritual formation.

That means we don't read the Bible through the lens of tradition alone, but through a living relationship with God. One of the clearest examples of this approach is how we engage with the reality that the Bible was written by men. And yet that doesn't mean it wasn't written *for* us. As Black women, we have every right to read, study, question, and breathe into these texts. A womanist lens becomes our compass—a framework that honors our culture, our womanhood, and our divine curiosity.

This year, we walk with God—with open hearts, steady steps, holy questions, and a roadmap we can trust.

WHAT MATERIALS DO I NEED?

This book.

The Bible. Use any version or translation you'd like. You may also benefit from an electronic or audio version that can be downloaded on your phone.

Notebook, journal, phone, tablet. This will be helpful if you want to take extra notes.

Pen or pencil.

WHAT'S IN THIS BOOK?

This devotional-style commentary is structured to help you read the entire Bible in one year—without overwhelm or guilt. Each of the 52 weeks includes six daily readings, followed by a seventh day reserved for rest, reflection, or catching up. The rhythm is intentional. We're not sprinting—we're walking. We're even honoring the Sabbath rhythm of rest that the Bible offers us.

Each week, I'll present a short devotional commentary designed to provide historical context, spiritual insight, and space to connect what's happening in that week's readings to experiences that may be unfolding in your own life. You'll also receive three reflective prompts (called "Sit with It") and a rotating bonus feature like Verse of the Week, Bible Truth, This I Pray, or Sis, Try This.

With approximately three chapters per day, you can expect the daily readings to take about 15 minutes. Some days might take longer. Some weeks might get messy. That's okay. This book was written with grace in mind. The point isn't perfection—it's presence.

Whether you're wrestling with doubt, reclaiming your faith, or simply longing to deepen your relationship with God, this devotional commentary is here to walk with you. Week by week, word by word, may you discover that Scripture doesn't just speak to your life—it holds it.

THE READING SCHEDULE

This reading plan moves through the Bible in a thoughtful order—not strictly from Genesis to Revelation. By weaving together Old and New Testament readings, you'll stay engaged during long sections of laws or lineage and enjoy the poetry of Psalms and Proverbs all year long. Each week's devotional connects to passages from that week or builds bridges across prior readings. Let the variety keep you motivated—and let the Holy Spirit guide you through the full story.

GREAT IN A GROUP OR ON YOUR OWN

Whether you're reading solo at sunrise or gathered with girlfriends one night a week, this book is designed to meet you where you are. Each week's prompts make great conversation starters for small groups, book clubs, Bible studies—or even the group chat. And if you're feeling called to lead, the Group Study Guide in the back provides extra support. However you choose to walk this journey, know this: You don't have to do it alone. May a sistah always be within reach.

YOU CAN DO IT!

Reading the Bible in a year might feel big—but so are you. Choose God. Choose yourself. Start with today. Then tomorrow. Keep going. Let grace fill the gaps. Over time, what once felt intimidating will start to feel familiar. You'll find rhythm. You'll find insight. You'll find yourself—more rooted in the Word, more grounded in God, and more at home with who God is calling you to be. Don't worry about being perfect. Just begin. Let's do this together.

WEEK 1

RECLAIM THE STORY

DAILY READINGS

- ☐ Day 1: Genesis 1–4
- ☐ Day 2: Genesis 5–8
- ☐ Day 3: Genesis 9–12
- ☐ Day 4: Genesis 13–15
- ☐ Day 5: Genesis 16–18
- ☐ Day 6: Genesis 19–21
- ☐ Day 7: Catch up on any readings you've missed.

MANY OF US KNOW what it's like to be unfairly labeled or even misunderstood. Like many Black girls, I was told I talked too much. In school, in church, even at home—my voice was labeled a distraction. I wasn't unruly, just expressive. Curious. Alive. But instead of encouragement, I got correction. Like Eve, I was misunderstood. But what they tried to manage was what God wanted to magnify. That same voice they tried to hush, God now uses to preach, teach, and tell the truth of Jesus—the truth that sets us free.

We meet Eve early in Genesis—and many of us have been taught to misjudge her since we were young. Eve has long been blamed as the reason for "the fall," the one who "messed it all up." However, what if we've misunderstood the most powerful part of her story?

In Genesis 3, we find Eve in conversation—not just with the serpent, but also with divine instruction itself. She recalls God's command, reflects on what was said, and then makes a choice. Many tell this story with emphasis on what Eve got wrong, but what if we paid closer attention to what she did first? She thought. She questioned. She discerned. She engaged in divine dialogue—and she did it out loud. That's why I refuse to call her weak. I want to boldly suggest Eve was the first interpreter of divine truth—the first to have the courage to wrestle with what God said *and* what it meant. That's not failure. That's formation.

Eve says, "We may eat fruit from the trees in the garden, but God did say, 'You must not eat fruit from the tree that is in the middle of the garden'" (Genesis 3:2–3). She remembers. She engages. She is trying to understand. We don't have to agree with her choice to recognize the sacredness of her seeking.

Her story has long been defined by the impact of the fall, but we rarely consider her intent. She wasn't trying to destroy paradise; she was trying to understand it. And although the consequences were serious, it was her disobedience toward God that was sinful, not her curiosity. Her curiosity was human, an early echo of our hunger to know the One who made us. Maybe even holy.

You, my sistah, are not defined by the assumptions of others. So go ahead. I dare you! Ask the questions. Speak the truth God placed within you. Because the God who walked with Eve in the garden is still walking with you.

SIT WITH IT

1. What assumptions have people made about you that aren't true?

2. How does Eve's courage to question resonate with your own story?

3. What story about yourself needs to be reframed in this season?

SIS, TRY THIS

1. Write down one mischaracterization that's been spoken over your life. As you pray over it, cross it out and then release it.
2. Then write what God says about you instead on a sticky note.
3. Affix it to your bathroom mirror and read it aloud every morning this week.

WEEK 2
A LESSON, NOT A LOSS

DAILY READINGS

- Day 1: Genesis 22–25
- Day 2: Genesis 26–29
- Day 3: Genesis 30–33
- Day 4: Genesis 34–36
- Day 5: Genesis 37–41
- Day 6: Genesis 42–46
- Day 7: Catch up on any readings you've missed.

BY NOW, YOU'VE READ ABOUT ABRAHAM—the one God promised would become a great nation—and Isaac, the quiet carrier of that covenant. Now, we arrive at Jacob: complex, cunning, called. He's a man marked by wrestling—first with his brother, then with his uncle, and now, finally, with himself.

In Genesis 32, Jacob is on the cusp of facing Esau, the brother he betrayed. He sends his family, his flocks, and everything he owns across the river, preparing for what could be a dangerous reunion. But Jacob stays behind. Alone. Restless. Wrestling not just with a stranger, but also with the weight of his past, the fear of what's ahead, and the question of who he truly is. The text says: "So Jacob was left alone, and a man wrestled with him till daybreak." (Genesis 32:24).

This divine encounter isn't about winning. It's about honesty. At one particular point, Jacob is asked to name himself, and he doesn't hide behind titles or excuses. He says, "Jacob"—the deceiver, the heel-grabber, the one who's always had to scheme. And God meets him right there. Not with shame, but with a blessing. Jacob walks away renamed: Israel—"one who wrestles with God." But he also walks away limping.

That limp is what makes this sacred. The limp isn't a punishment—it's a reminder. A sign that transformation costs something. It's what happens when we stop pretending and start telling the truth about who we've been and who we're becoming.

Sometimes the wrestling in our own lives shows up after a friendship ends. When someone we loved deeply becomes a stranger. When we're left sorting through the pieces—grief, guilt, silence. Real friendships don't define us, but they help refine us. And when they're gone, the ache is real.

I've been there. Holding on. Replaying conversations. Wishing I could change the ending. But the truth is that eventually I had to stop fighting to preserve what God was asking me to release. Through time, prayer, and therapy, letting go didn't feel like winning—it felt like limping.

Sistah, if you're walking with a limp after losing a friendship that mattered, let me remind you: You're still walking. You didn't lose. You learned. The limp is just proof that you've wrestled—and come out blessed.

SIT WITH IT

1. Have you ever experienced the loss of a friendship that felt like losing family? How did that shift your understanding of trust or connection?

2. What is something or someone you've physically let go of, but still carry in your heart, your body, or your spirit?

3. What "limp" do you carry from a past season of grief or struggle? What has it taught you about who you are now?

THIS I PRAY

God, help me release what's too heavy to carry. Teach me to trust that my limp is not a sign of weakness, but a mark of transformation. Remind me that even in my aching places, I am still moving—and you are still walking with me. Amen.

WEEK 3

SACRED DISOBEDIENCE

DAILY READINGS

- ☐ Day 1: Genesis 47–50
- ☐ Day 2: Exodus 1–3
- ☐ Day 3: Exodus 4–7
- ☐ Day 4: Exodus 8–11
- ☐ Day 5: Exodus 12–15
- ☐ Day 6: Exodus 16–18
- ☐ Day 7: Catch up on any readings you've missed.

BEFORE MOSES WAS CALLED, before a sea was split, before Pharaoh's army drowned, two women had the courage to risk it all with a "no." And let's be honest: Black women have always had the courage to say no.

In Exodus 1:15–22, the Hebrew midwives Shiphrah and Puah are living under harsh Egyptian oppression. Pharaoh, fearful that the growing Israelite population might rise up, orders the women to kill every Hebrew boy at birth. The pressure is high. The punishment is certain. And still, these women choose another way. No public protest. No speech. Just a quiet, deliberate refusal to participate in injustice.

This passage shows us what it means to fear God more than Pharaoh. Truth is, they likely feared both, but their fear turned into a faith that saved a generation. Their "no" may have looked like defiance in the eyes of the world, but in God's eyes, it was deliverance. Their courage created room for Moses, and for a future far bigger than their present.

As little girls, many of us were taught that obedience made us "good." We were praised for compliance, for keeping the peace, for avoiding disruption. But becoming a grown woman of faith often means learning the difference between blind obedience and sacred resistance. Obedience may be for a season, but sacred disobedience? That's for when wisdom and courage grow strong enough to walk together.

Ella Baker understood this. She wasn't always front and center, but her influence ran deep. Known as the "Mother of the Civil Rights Movement," she mentored young activists, challenged the idea that leadership had to look like one charismatic man, and helped birth movements rooted in grassroots power. She didn't wait for permission to protect life or shape the future. She simply did the work. Quietly. Consistently. Courageously.

In a world where men have often had the loudest voices, Ella, Shiphrah, and Puah—and women like them—teach us something different: You don't need to hold the mic to hold the line.

Let me be clear: Sacred disobedience isn't about rebellion for rebellion's sake. It's about choosing what's right when the consequences are real. It starts in the shadows, in quiet rooms, in systems where silence is expected.

You may not think your choices matter. But I'm here to remind you that they do.

Sistah, your "no" is holy. Your refusal can be righteous. Your quiet resistance might be the very thing that changes everything.

SIT WITH IT

1. How were you taught to define obedience growing up? How is that definition evolving as your faith deepens and matures?

2. When have you been asked to stay silent or compliant, but felt called to say no instead? What did it cost you—and what did it teach you?

3. Who are the women in your family, church, or community whose quiet resistance shaped your survival?

BIBLE TRUTH

Shiphrah and Puah are the first named individuals in the book of Exodus—before Moses, before Pharaoh. Their names, which mean "beauty" and "splendor," are preserved in Scripture as a testament to the power of quiet resistance. Their placement at the very beginning of Exodus signals that liberation begins not with power or spectacle, but with women who fear God and choose life in small, courageous ways.

WEEK 4
ASK ANYWAY

DAILY READINGS

- Day 1: Exodus 19–21
- Day 2: Exodus 22–25
- Day 3: Exodus 26–29
- Day 4: Exodus 30–32
- Day 5: Exodus 33–36
- Day 6: Exodus 37–40
- Day 7: Catch up on any readings you've missed.

BY NOW, YOU'VE SEEN Moses advocate for God's people, climb the mountain to receive instruction, and come back down only to find chaos and betrayal. He's carried spiritual responsibility, disappointment, and fatigue. Now—in Exodus 33—he dares to ask for something that could change everything.

"Show me your glory," he says in Exodus 33:18. It's a bold prayer, and it comes from an exhausted place. Moses isn't just tired; he's spiritually depleted. God has just told him, "I'll send an angel to go with you, but I won't go myself." That's when Moses hits a breaking point. He pushes back on God and pleads for more than survival. Moses wants presence. Assurance. Closeness. He dares to ask anyway.

This is a prayer for the worn out—for the ones who are expected to carry it all and still keep going.

Black women know that weight intimately. Around 80 percent of Black mothers are the primary or sole breadwinners in their homes. Many are raising children and caring for aging parents. Despite holding the highest number of graduate degrees per capita of any group of women, Black women are still paid less than every major demographic in the workforce.

We are overextended and under-supported. Told to be strong but not sensitive. Grateful but not needy. Capable but not critical.

Several years ago, I was in a season where everything felt like too much—marriage, motherhood, work, supporting family, making sure my mother had what she needed. I was managing everything but myself. One Saturday, I stood in my kitchen cooking a pot of collard greens for Sunday dinner, and I felt this wave of sacred presence surround me—like generations of Black women who had carried too much were right there with me. That day, I reached my breaking point. Over that pot, as I seasoned those greens, I whispered a simple prayer: "God, make me more effective."

It wasn't loud. It wasn't detailed or specific or eloquent. But it was real. I believe God heard me that day. Everything began to shift—not comfortably, but intentionally. Today, I am sitting in the fruit of that ask.

So when Moses asks to see God's glory, I understand. God doesn't shame him. God shelters him. Thank goodness, God meets tired people with tenderness.

Sistah, your tired body, your busy mind, your bruised heart—even your weary spirit—they're all still holy enough to hold a bold ask.

I dare you: *Ask anyway.*

SIT WITH IT

1. When was the last time you asked God for something bold—not because you felt strong, but because you were tired?

2. What responsibilities are you carrying right now that feel heavy but holy? How are they affecting your spirit?

3. What would it look like to pray, not for more strength, but for more of God's presence in the middle of your exhaustion?

THIS I PRAY

Awesome and mighty God, I'm carrying more than I have words for right now and I'm tired in places no one sees. Yet today, I come to You—with not a polished ask, but a real one. Please, show me Your presence. Remind me that I don't have to carry it all alone. Where I am weary, come close. Where I am empty, fill me. Let my exhausted yet simple prayer be enough. Let Your glory meet me at every turn this week. In Jesus's name, amen.

WEEK 5

GOD STILL USED HER

DAILY READINGS

- Day 1: Matthew 1–3
- Day 2: Matthew 4–7
- Day 3: Matthew 8–11
- Day 4: Matthew 12–15
- Day 5: Matthew 16–19
- Day 6: Matthew 20–22
- Day 7: Catch up on any readings you've missed.

IF YOU'VE EVER FELT like your story disqualifies you—like you've made too many mistakes or taken too many wrong turns—then, my sistah, Matthew 1 was written with you in mind.

Matthew begins with a genealogy—a long list of names most people skip. But nestled in that list are five women: Tamar, Rahab, Ruth, Bathsheba, and Mary. And their inclusion is no accident.

Tamar was widowed twice and denied justice by the very family that was supposed to protect her. So she risked her reputation and disguised herself to confront injustice face to face (Genesis 38). Rahab was a Canaanite and a sex worker who had the spiritual insight to protect God's people and claim a new legacy (Joshua 2). Her name reappears in Hebrews 11:31 as a woman of faith.

Ruth was a Moabite—an outsider in both bloodline and belonging—who chose loyalty over security. Her boldness and steadfastness led her into the line of kings. Bathsheba, named only by association to her first husband, Uriah, was drawn into David's abuse of power. But through her, Solomon—the wisest king—was born, and her presence in the lineage signals restoration after harm.

And Mary? A young, unmarried, and pregnant girl—who would give birth to a miracle no one would believe. She bore the weight of divine calling with courage and consent.

None of these women were what society would've called "ideal." Each of them had a story that brought whispers, shame, or judgment. And yet God said: *Write her in.* Let this serve as a reminder: Your identity is not defined by what's been done to you, or even by what you've done. What others would discard, God documents. Not to embarrass you, but to affirm that you belong in the lineage of promise.

Every woman has a story. And I'd guess there are parts of yours—decisions, detours, disappointments—that you've wondered if God could use. But here's the truth: God wastes nothing. Sometimes what looks like delay is actually divine development. Ruth didn't know loyalty would lead to legacy. Mary didn't know her "yes" would change the world.

Give God time and opportunity to redeem what feels uncertain, and to reveal why the story had to unfold the way it did.

Sistah, don't rush to erase your "outsider" story. God may be writing you in. You are not a sidenote. You are part of the strategy.

SIT WITH IT

1. Which woman in Jesus's genealogy do you most identify with and why?

2. Have you ever felt excluded because of a decision you made or something done to you? What would it mean to believe God still includes you?

3. What part of your story have you tried to hide that God might want to use?

BIBLE TRUTH

Rahab, one of the five women listed in Jesus's genealogy, was not only a Canaanite and sex worker—she was also the great-great-grandmother of King David. Her story proves that your past doesn't disqualify you—and neither does your bloodline. God's promise makes room for you too.

WEEK 6

CARRYING THE GOOD NEWS

DAILY READINGS

- Day 1: Matthew 23–25
- Day 2: Matthew 26–28
- Day 3: Leviticus 1–4
- Day 4: Leviticus 5–8
- Day 5: Leviticus 9–12
- Day 6: Leviticus 13–15
- Day 7: Catch up on any readings you've missed.

BY NOW, YOU'VE READ how Matthew begins his Gospel—not with royal men or polished leaders, but with five women whose lives were complicated. Tamar. Rahab. Ruth. Bathsheba. Mary. Each had a story that would have made people raise their eyebrows. But God chose to include them—not as footnotes, but as part of the foundation.

And now, in Matthew 28, at the very end of the Gospel, we see the same intention: God still entrusts women with something sacred. Mary Magdalene and the other Mary rise early, at dawn, and go to the tomb carrying spices to anoint Jesus's body. They come grieving, not expecting resurrection—but still, they show up. Their love drives them to the last known place they saw Him. And it's there, when grief and devotion collide, that heaven responds. An angel appears in dazzling white, rolls the stone away, and says: "He is not here; he has risen, just as he said" (Matthew 28:6). The women don't hesitate. Scripture indicates they are afraid yet filled with joy as they run to tell the disciples. And it's on that very path that Jesus meets them.

He greets them tenderly and reaffirms their mission: "Do not be afraid. Go and tell my brothers to go to Galilee; there they will see me" (Matthew 28:10).

The first voices to proclaim the resurrection weren't priests or prophets. They were women. Not because they were flawless, but because they were faithful.

Let's talk about Mary Magdalene. Scripture tells us she was once delivered from seven demons. People probably whispered her name like it was a scandal. Some likely questioned why Jesus kept her so near. But when it came time to carry the good news, she was the one Jesus trusted. That should tell us something important: Just because people doubt your worth doesn't mean God does. Suspicion may be real, but it's not divine. The world may label you "unfit," but heaven refers to you as "called."

That's the arc of Matthew. The Gospel begins with women who had a past, and the resurrection is first revealed to a woman who had a past. From start to finish, Matthew shows us that God uses women. Period.

So, my sister—if you've ever felt judged, overlooked, or unworthy because of your story, take heart. God can still trust you with something holy. Your past is not too messy. Your presence still matters. You, too, can carry the good news.

SIT WITH IT

1. Mary Magdalene showed up despite her grief, fear, and past. What do you think gave her the strength to be present at the tomb? What might help you show up more fully in your own life, even when it's hard?

2. Reflect on a time when someone judged your past or questioned your calling. How did it shape the way you see yourself? How might God be inviting you to see yourself differently now?

3. Is there a part of your story you've considered disqualifying? How might God use that very thing to help someone else? What does it mean to you to believe your presence is a ministry?

THIS I PRAY

Awesome and mighty God, thank You for seeing me—not through the lens of my past, but through the lens of Your purpose. When others only see where I've been, You see where I'm going. Help me stand in my full story—not with shame, but with strength. Give me the courage to carry what's sacred, even when I feel unqualified, unseen, or unsure. Let my presence be my "yes," and let my "yes" lead someone else to hope. In Jesus's name, amen.

WEEK 7

YOU DESERVE TO STOP

DAILY READINGS

- Day 1: Psalms 1–3
- Day 2: Leviticus 16–19
- Day 3: Leviticus 20–23
- Day 4: Psalms 4–6
- Day 5: Leviticus 24–27
- Day 6: Psalms 7–10
- Day 7: Catch up on any readings you've missed.

IF THERE'S ONE THING Black women have mastered, it's holding it all together. We are often the backbone—at home, at work, in church, within our families, and in our communities. So it's no surprise that in Leviticus 23, before God gives instructions about holy festivals—moments where women likely carried much of the unseen labor—God offers one command: Rest. Sabbath isn't optional. It's not a reward for finishing your to-do list. It's not a luxury reserved for the wealthy or retired. Sabbath is a divine requirement—an invitation to trust that the world will keep turning even when you choose to stop.

In 2022, I was awarded a Lilly Foundation grant that allowed me to step away from ministry for twelve weeks. I traveled. I rested. I listened deeply to God, and to myself. And do you know what I learned? The world didn't fall apart in my absence. My work was still there. My family was still cared for. Life kept moving, and I returned more whole than I had been in years.

That time away also taught me boundaries. It taught me how to say no, and that pouring into my own cup isn't selfish—it's survival. In fact, a major opportunity I had long prayed for came during that Sabbath season. It tested my "no," but I offered it by faith. No, I didn't get that opportunity again in 2023—but in 2024, the invitation returned. And this time, the timing was right, and I was rested.

You've heard it on every flight: Put your own oxygen mask on first. But for many of us—especially Black women—that's not our instinct. It has to become our practice. After one Sabbath workshop, a woman approached me. She was a caregiver for her mother, overworked and under-supported. "How do I find Sabbath?" she asked.

I told her to start with one hour. Not for errands. Not for maintenance. One hour to breathe, create, or rest. A year later, she'd expanded that hour to four each week. She told me it changed her life and helped her hold others accountable by protecting that time with her "no."

Rest is where I reclaim myself, where I lay down my superwoman cape and whisper, "God, I trust You to hold it." Sabbath makes space for God to pour back into what we've poured out.

Hear me clearly, sis: You don't have to earn rest. You were created for it. You deserve to stop. I dare you to try.

SIT WITH IT

1. What messages—from family, culture, or faith—have shaped your relationship with rest? Have those messages helped you or harmed you? What do you think God might be inviting you to unlearn?

2. Think about your current rhythm of life. Where are you pouring out the most? Where do you need God to pour back into you?

3. What is a boundary you can set this week to protect your rest? Whether it's carving out one uninterrupted hour or saying no to something that drains you, name one action you'll take to honor Sabbath in your own life.

SIS, TRY THIS

Set aside one hour this week for sacred rest. Don't use it to clean, catch up, or check in. Use it to breathe, to be still, to be with God. Light incense, take a walk, sit in silence, write in your journal—whatever reminds you that the world can wait. Then, reflect: How did that one hour shift your spirit?

WEEK 8
WISDOM IS A WOMAN

DAILY READINGS

- Day 1: Numbers 1–4
- Day 2: Numbers 5–6
- Day 3: Proverbs 1–3
- Day 4: Numbers 7–9
- Day 5: Numbers 10–13
- Day 6: Proverbs 4–7
- Day 7: Catch up on any readings you've missed.

IF YOU'VE EVER DOUBTED your discernment or silenced your own knowing, Proverbs reminds us: Wisdom is a woman. And she is not quiet: "Out in the open wisdom calls aloud, she raises her voice in the public square; on top of the wall she cries out, at the city gate she makes her speech" (Proverbs 1:20–21). Not in secret. Not hidden in ivory towers or in back rooms. Wisdom is out loud and in public—just like you may need to be.

In the Hebrew text, *Chokmah* (wisdom) is a feminine noun, and her personification as a woman is both poetic and profound. Wisdom is not only nurturing but life-giving; not only discerning but decisive. Some theologians believe this feminine depiction offers a glimpse into the inclusive and multifaceted nature of God, who creates, guides, births, and builds.

Womanist theology—rooted in the lived experience of Black women and their faith—takes this further. Womanist scholars remind us that the wisdom we inherit isn't only intellectual. It's ancestral, embodied, and spiritual. It is passed through mothers, mentors, memory, and the Holy Spirit.

Black women have always known things before the world was ready to listen. And our wisdom has never been just personal—it has been political, prophetic, and public. I think of the late Judye Thomas, a Freedom Rider and legend in my denomination. She didn't just speak wisdom—she embodied it. She laid her body in front of box store trucks to protect local farmers. Her voice for justice was so bold that she landed on the federal no-fly list—and she wore it like a badge of honor. Her wisdom changed her community because she dared to bring it to the streets.

Wisdom doesn't always whisper politely. Sometimes she disrupts, dismantles, and declares a new way forward. Her voice may unsettle those invested in silence, but that is the point. She is meant to shake the ground until justice takes root and liberation takes shape.

Scripture doesn't just describe wisdom—it blesses her: "She is more precious than rubies... a tree of life to those who take hold of her; those who hold her fast will be blessed" (Proverbs 3:15, 18).

Sistah, when you hear the Spirit say "speak up," don't ignore her. When you sense the nudge that something isn't right, listen. That's wisdom—your divine inheritance. Let her speak through you. You are wisdom walking.

SIT WITH IT

1. When have you silenced your own wisdom? What kept you quiet, and what would it look like to speak up now?

2. How does seeing wisdom as a woman—loud, public, and sacred—shift how you understand your voice and value?

3. What is one area in your life where you feel wisdom nudging you to act or speak? What's stopping you?

VERSE OF THE WEEK

Out in the open wisdom calls aloud, she raises her voice in the public square.

Proverbs 1:20

WEEK 9

WHEN GRIEF GOES UNSPOKEN

DAILY READINGS

- [ ] Day 1: Numbers 14–16
- [ ] Day 2: Numbers 17–19
- [ ] Day 3: Numbers 20–22
- [ ] Day 4: Proverbs 8–11
- [ ] Day 5: Numbers 23–26
- [ ] Day 6: Proverbs 12–14
- [ ] Day 7: Catch up on any readings you've missed.

WE STEP INTO NUMBERS 20 at a painful moment: Miriam has died. Moses's sister—the one who watched over him in the Nile and stood beside him in liberation—is gone. But there is no pause to grieve. The people begin complaining again. There's no water. Tensions rise. And Moses is once again expected to lead like everything's fine.

But he's not fine. He's grief-stricken. And unspoken grief has a way of becoming dangerous when it goes untended.

God tells him to speak to the rock. Instead, he strikes it—twice. The water flows, but the cost is steep. Then God says: "Because you did not trust in me enough to honor me as holy in the sight of the Israelites, you will not bring this community into the land I give them" (Numbers 20:12).

This wasn't just ordinary frustration. This was sorrow showing up sideways. It was a moment to trust God when Moses knew he didn't have it in him. A moment when he knew he wasn't at his best. But instead of surrendering to that truth, he acted like everything was business as usual—and it cost him.

Proverbs 14:10 says, "Each heart knows its own bitterness." God knew Moses's heart was heavy. And instead of rewarding his self-denial, God called him to more trust—not performance.

I've lived this. When my father died, I tried to be strong for everyone—my mother, my newly pregnant sister, my uncle. I preached my father's eulogy and kept going. But eventually, my body collapsed. I landed in the hospital with internal complications. My body said what my mouth wouldn't: *I am not okay*.

Since then, I've learned to grieve differently. To serve from the Lord's strength, not my own overcompensation. I've put better boundaries in place. I now see falling apart as not a failure, but as part of healing.

Because here's what I know now: God is not just present in our power. God meets us in our pain. And sometimes, the most faithful thing you can do is admit: *I need help. I need rest. I need time.*

Sistah, if you've been showing up while silencing your sorrow, take this as your permission: You don't have to strike the rock. You can stop. You can trust God to hold what's too heavy for you to carry. You were never meant to grieve in silence.

SIT WITH IT

1. Miriam's death is mentioned in a single verse, and the story quickly moves on. Have you ever experienced a loss that felt rushed or unacknowledged? How did it impact the way you processed your grief?

2. Think about a time when you, like Moses, reacted from a place of unspoken sorrow or fatigue. What might have helped you name your pain sooner?

3. What grief are you carrying that needs space to be seen, spoken, or surrendered? What would it look like to trust God with that weight today?

THIS, I PRAY

God, I've been holding a lot—some things too heavy to name. Today, I give You what's underneath my strength. Meet me in the places I've kept quiet. Give me grace to grieve and trust to rest. Remind me that I don't have to hold it all because You hold me. I trust You with my heart. In Jesus's name, amen.

WEEK 10

CHANGE THE SEATING CHART

DAILY READINGS

- Day 1: Numbers 27–30
- Day 2: Numbers 31–33
- Day 3: Numbers 34–36
- Day 4: Mark 1–5
- Day 5: Mark 6–10
- Day 6: Mark 11–16
- Day 7: Catch up on any readings you've missed.

WHAT DOES IT MEAN to walk into a room and advocate for what's rightfully yours? To steady your voice even when it shakes? To hold your ground? To ask with confidence, even when tradition says you shouldn't? Sistah, that moment is familiar to many of us. Whether it's negotiating a salary, fighting for equity, requesting what's owed to you, or refusing to be overlooked—we know what it means to stand up and ask anyway.

The daughters of Zelophehad, who are introduced in Numbers 27, knew it too. Their father had died with no sons to carry his name. As women without husbands or sons to represent them, they were expected to forfeit their family's inheritance. By custom, the land would likely pass to distant male relatives or be confiscated by leadership—but certainly not be given to women.

Still, Mahlah, Noah, Hoglah, Milkah, and Tirzah stood up and said: No. Not this time. Not on our watch. They didn't beg. They didn't plead. They made a righteous case not just for themselves, but for every woman to come. They had the courage to set a precedent.

And here's what still stuns me: God sided with the women. It wasn't the men, the elders, or the system that declared them right. God did. God affirmed their boldness. God rewrote the policy. God saw the courage it took to walk into a room where they were outnumbered—and still ask. In Numbers 27:7, God tells Moses, "What Zelophehad's daughters are saying is right. You must certainly give them property as an inheritance among their father's relatives and give their father's inheritance to them." In that moment, God doesn't just hear their request; God honors it. Their courage becomes the catalyst for systemic change.

As Shirley Chisholm once said, "If they don't give you a seat at the table, bring a folding chair." She spoke those words as the first Black woman elected to the United States Congress—a woman who had been excluded, underestimated, and overlooked. Her statement wasn't just about politics; it was about presence and persistence.

These sisters didn't just bring their chairs—they changed the seating chart for generations to come.

So if your voice shakes but you still speak; if your hands tremble but you still type the email, make the call, or take the meeting; and if you've ever had to demand what you know is just, then you are walking in the spirit of Zelophehad's daughters. You're not being difficult. You're being strategic—by faith.

Sistah, don't second-guess the power of your ask. God may be getting ready to say: She's right.

SIT WITH IT

1. What are the "tables" in your life—spaces where decisions are made—that you've been hesitant to approach? What stops you? What might shift if you showed up with confidence and clarity?

2. The daughters of Zelophehad didn't just speak for themselves—they changed the system for future women. Where in your life or work might your boldness today open doors for others tomorrow?

3. This week, ask God to strengthen your voice. Write out one thing you need to speak up about in your family, career, ministry, or personal life. What would it look like to make your case with courage and trust that God will back you up?

BIBLE TRUTH

The daughters of Zelophehad were the first women in the Bible to initiate a legal claim for inheritance, and God affirmed their request. Numbers 27:7 says: "What Zelophehad's daughters are saying is right." This moment sets a biblical precedent for equity and shows that righteous advocacy is not only heard by God; it is honored by God.

WEEK 11

FROM SURVIVING TO SETTLING

DAILY READINGS

- Day 1: Deuteronomy 1–4
- Day 2: Deuteronomy 5–8
- Day 3: Psalms 11–14
- Day 4: Deuteronomy 9–11
- Day 5: Deuteronomy 12–15
- Day 6: Psalms 15–17
- Day 7: Catch up on any readings you've missed.

BY NOW, YOU'VE SEEN Israel come a long way. After years of wandering, hunger, and hard lessons, God gives them a charge in Deuteronomy 8—not to forget how they got here. God reminds them that the wilderness wasn't just a holding place—it was a teaching ground. God didn't abandon them there; God fed them there. God shaped their dependence. Their hunger was met with manna, and their struggle was laced with sacred lessons. Through this wilderness journey, one thing is made abundantly clear: God was faithful in their wilderness experience.

Now, flash forward to the testimony in Psalm 16. Here, a similar sentiment is echoed around God's faithfulness—but this time, it's not in a wilderness setting. Instead, it's the reflection of someone who's made it to the other side. Unlike Deuteronomy 8, this Psalm isn't about survival—it's about settlement: "Lord, you alone are my portion and my cup; you make my lot secure. The boundary lines have fallen for me in pleasant places; surely I have a delightful inheritance" (Psalm 16:5–6).

The same God who carried the Israelites through the wilderness in Deuteronomy also secured their portion. The fight was never about scarcity; it was about faith—faith in the God who feeds, provides, positions, and protects. The wilderness taught God's people to trust. Now the inheritance invites them to rest.

Sistah, if you're coming out of a long season of survival—where you had to do too much with too little—let this be your reminder: That season didn't define you. It prepared you.

Our ancestors understood this kind of trust in the faithfulness of God, no matter the season. Harriet Tubman didn't have maps or guarantees, but she had memory of how God delivered before, and she let that memory guide her obedience. Sometimes the only way forward is to remember what God has already brought you through. We must hold on to the seasons we've come through—those moments when we could finally declare: "The boundary lines have fallen for me in pleasant places."

Never forget: Memory becomes the soil where trust grows. Your grandmother's prayers, your mother's perseverance, your own past victories—these are not just stories. They are proof that God made a way then, and God will do it again.

Maybe you're in a season where God is drawing new lines, granting fresh peace, or inviting you to receive what you once had to fight for. Let God bless you. The God who met you in survival is the same God who sustains you in settlement.

SIT WITH IT

1. What "wilderness" season have you survived that taught you how to trust God differently?

2. How do you know when it's time to receive instead of strive?

3. What is a memory you have of God's past faithfulness? How can you use this to build trust for the season you're in?

SIS, TRY THIS

Set a ten-minute timer and write down five moments when God showed up for you. Keep the list visible. Let it remind you: God will do it again.

WEEK 12

LET GOD LEAD YOU

DAILY READINGS

- Day 1: Deuteronomy 16–18
- Day 2: Deuteronomy 19–21
- Day 3: Psalms 18–21
- Day 4: Deuteronomy 22–25
- Day 5: Deuteronomy 26–28
- Day 6: Psalms 22–25
- Day 7: Catch up on any readings you've missed.

IF THERE'S ONE THING Black women are often taught, it's how to carry a heavy load. It's ingrained in us from childhood. We shoulder emotional labor, household burdens, other people's expectations. In fact, a 2017 Georgetown Law study found that Black girls as young as five are seen as more adultlike, more responsible, and less in need of nurturing than their white peers. We are handed the strength of womanhood before we're offered the softness of girlhood. We learn to survive before we're invited to trust.

Yet this idea is lovingly confronted in Psalm 23, where we are given something radical: the image of a Shepherd who leads—and a promise that following is safe. "The Lord is my shepherd, I lack nothing" (Psalm 23:1).

Psalm 23 was written by David—a shepherd turned king—who knew what it meant to lead and to be led. He likely penned these words in reflection after watching how God guided him through danger, loss, and transition. This Psalm is not a declaration of triumph—it's a confession of trust. It reminds us peace doesn't come from position; it comes from presence—God's presence.

As a single mother, this verse has become my lifeline. There were months I wasn't sure how to make one income stretch far enough. Nights when I looked at my child, the bills, and my own exhaustion and thought: *I don't have what it takes.* But I kept repeating those words: "I lack nothing." Not because the numbers added up—but because the Shepherd showed up. My oil has run low, but let me testify, it has never run dry.

And when life surrounded me with pressure, loss, or fear, God set the table anyway. "You prepare a table before me in the presence of my enemies" (Psalm 23:5).

That's not just provision—that's protection. That's a full-circle kind of faith. The kind where the same God who walked with you through the valley seats you in a place of peace, right where the pain used to live.

Goodness and mercy? They're not distant ideas. They're divine companions. They've followed me even when I wasn't sure where I was going. They've covered me when I couldn't cover myself.

Sistah, I know it's hard to let go. Hard to rest. Hard to be led when you've been in charge for so long. But what if the next chapter of your life isn't about holding it all together, but trusting the One who's holding you?

You don't have to earn peace. You don't have to force the blessing. Let God lead you, and I promise you'll lack nothing.

SIT WITH IT

1. Where in your life have you been leading out of obligation, instead of letting God lead you with peace and trust?

2. What does "I lack nothing" mean to you in this season—emotionally, spiritually, or financially?

3. How might you redefine strength as surrender instead of striving?

BIBLE TRUTH

Psalm 23 is one of the most widely memorized and quoted Scriptures in the Bible. It was written by David, who had firsthand experience as a shepherd—making his description of God's care deeply personal and profound. Found early in the Book of Psalms, it is written as a continuous piece of poetry. Its wording has endured across cultures, languages, and time.

WEEK 13

COURAGE TO CROSS OVER

DAILY READINGS

- Day 1: Deuteronomy 29–31
- Day 2: Deuteronomy 32–34
- Day 3: Joshua 1–4
- Day 4: Joshua 5–8
- Day 5: Joshua 9–12
- Day 6: Joshua 13–16
- Day 7: Catch up on any readings you've missed.

BY THE TIME YOU finish reading Deuteronomy 34, you likely feel the weight of a shifting moment. Moses—the towering leader who walked the people out of Egypt, up Mount Sinai, and through the wilderness—is gone. Grief is in the air. Transition is at hand. A baton is passing.

Now, in Joshua 1, God turns to the one who must lead the Israelites next—Moses's longtime assistant, Joshua. And God doesn't waste words:

"Be strong and courageous" (Joshua 1:6).

"Be strong and very courageous" (Joshua 1:7).

"Be strong and courageous. Do not be afraid; do not be discouraged, for the Lord your God will be with you wherever you go" (Joshua 1:9).

That repetition isn't just encouragement—it's instruction. God knew what Joshua was about to step into: unfamiliar terrain, untested leadership, unpredictable people. This was not a moment for self-confidence. This was a call to divine trust. Strength is not what Joshua had to *possess*—it's what he had to *choose to trust.*

What's even more striking is the positioning of this command: Joshua is told to be courageous *before* the crossover—before he leads, before the Jordan parts, before Jericho falls. Courage isn't the result of progress. It's the posture required to begin.

And the command isn't given in a vacuum—it's anchored in a promise: "The Lord your God will be with you wherever you go" (Joshua 1:9). Everything turns on that truth. Joshua isn't being sent into uncertainty alone. God's presence is the reason courage is possible. The strength isn't about Joshua—it's about God.

When I became the pastor of my congregation, I was the first woman, the first African American, and the youngest to hold the position in its nearly two hundred-year history. I was scared. I knew what I represented—but I also knew what I lacked. And in those early days, titles didn't sustain me—trust in God did. I had to do it scared. I had to take courage. And the truth is, that's been the most significant part of my sustainability—not confidence in myself, but confidence in the One who called me.

This moment in Scripture reminds us that we can be both *uncertain* and *anointed.* That courage and fear can coexist, and that faith is not the absence of fear, but the decision to move forward anyway.

Sistah, if you're standing at the edge of a new season—a calling, a decision, a change—hear this: You are not empty-handed. You have a charge. You have instruction. And most of all, you have God.

It's time to cross over.

SIT WITH IT

1. What transition or new territory are you currently standing at the edge of? How is God inviting you to step forward in courage?

2. Reread Joshua 1:6–9. What does God's repetition of "Be strong and courageous" reveal about the emotions Joshua might have been holding?

3. In what areas of your life have you been relying on titles or credentials instead of trusting God's presence?

THIS I PRAY

God, You see what I'm standing in front of and what I'm carrying behind me. Thank You for reminding me that I don't need to be fearless—just faithful. Give me the strength to move forward even when I'm afraid. Help me trust that You go before me, walk beside me, and cover me from behind. Where I hesitate, fill me with courage. Where I'm weary, remind me that You are with me. It's time to cross over—and I trust You to lead the way. Amen.

WEEK 14

WHEN THE CALL DOESN'T MAKE SENSE

DAILY READINGS

- Day 1: Joshua 17–20
- Day 2: Joshua 21–24
- Day 3: Proverbs 15–17
- Day 4: Judges 1–3
- Day 5: Judges 4–6
- Day 6: Judges 7–10
- Day 7: Catch up on any readings you've missed.

YOU MIGHT HAVE NOTICED by now a familiar pattern: The Israelites disobey, find themselves oppressed, cry out to God, and are rescued through someone God raises up. That someone, in this case, is Deborah—and she doesn't fit the mold. She is not what they were expecting. At a time when leadership was typically male, Deborah stands out not just because she's a woman, but because she holds authority, discernment, and divine appointment.

Judges were not kings or priests. They were leaders raised up by God to guide, protect, and deliver the people. And Deborah? She's the only woman in the entire book of Judges who holds this role. Not only is she a prophet, she's also a military leader and the one people come to for wisdom and direction. At a time when women weren't seen as public leaders, Deborah is a judge over all of Israel. Her leadership is spiritual, political, and prophetic—and it's legitimate.

Then there's Gideon, who arrives on the scene in Judges 6. Unlike Deborah, Gideon doesn't step into leadership with confidence. He doubts his own strength, questions God's presence, and begs for signs that the call is real—twice demanding miracles with a fleece: first drenched with dew while the ground stayed dry, then dry while the ground was wet. Yet God still calls him. Why? Because in both cases—whether confident or conflicted—God chooses whom God chooses.

My preaching colleagues and I often say: "God doesn't call the equipped—God equips the called." It's not just a saying; it's a testimony. We serve a God who prepares us as we go.

Sistah, maybe you've been questioning the call on your life. Maybe the titles, tools, or timing don't seem to add up. Maybe you're looking around wondering, "Why me?" But here's what Deborah and Gideon both prove: You don't need to have it all together to be chosen. You just need a willing heart and a "yes."

God tells Gideon, "Go in the strength you have... Am I not sending you?" (Judges 6:14). That's all the confirmation we need.

Your call doesn't have to look like someone else's. It just has to sound like obedience.

So whether you're stepping up with boldness like Deborah or stepping in with hesitation like Gideon, know this: God's call still stands. You may not feel ready, but you're already seen. You're already called. And God will meet you in the going.

SIT WITH IT

1. Think about a time you were called to lead or serve in a role that didn't feel "fitting." How did you respond?

2. Which story of leadership do you relate to more right now—Deborah's confidence or Gideon's caution? Why?

3. Where might God be calling you to go in the strength you already have?

BIBLE TRUTH

In Judges 4, Jael—a woman living in alliance with Israel—plays a surprising and pivotal role in their victory over the Canaanite army. When the Canaanite general Sisera flees the battlefield, he hides in Jael's tent. She offers him hospitality—and then drives a tent peg through his head while he sleeps (Judges 4:21). Her unexpected bravery fulfills Deborah's prophecy in verse 9: "The Lord will deliver Sisera into the hands of a woman."

WEEK 15

WHEN THE BIBLE BREAKS YOUR HEART

DAILY READINGS

- [ ] Day 1: Judges 11–14
- [ ] Day 2: Judges 15–17
- [ ] Day 3: Judges 18–21
- [ ] Day 4: Psalms 26–29
- [ ] Day 5: Psalms 30–33
- [ ] Day 6: Psalms 34–37
- [ ] Day 7: Catch up on any readings you've missed.

Note to Readers: As we continue through the book of Judges, we encounter some of Scripture's most painful stories. These accounts include sexual violence and deep trauma. It's okay to pause, breathe, or skip ahead if you need to.

IN JUDGES 11, JEPHTHAH sacrifices his daughter after a careless vow in an effort to win a battle. In Judges 19, a woman is assaulted and discarded in the most brutal way. These stories are horrific. And the most haunting part? There's no clear justice. No divine interruption. Just silence, sorrow, and systemic failure.

Biblical scholar and feminist theologian Phyllis Trible calls these "texts of terror." They don't console—they confront. And we are right to be disturbed, maybe even heartbroken, by this sacred text.

What makes these stories even more unsettling is how normalized the violence becomes. Jephthah's vow goes unchallenged. The Levite barely grieves the woman who saved his life. Her pain is unnamed; her death, unpunished. These aren't just moments of personal failure—they reveal a wider moral collapse. Women's bodies are treated as expendable, and the narrative moves on without consequence.

So how do we sit with Scripture that seems to betray its own values?

First, we name the truth. These women's stories were recorded, but their voices were not. Their suffering is not the will of God—it is a warning about what happens when people ignore divine justice. Judges ends with a painful indictment: "everyone did as they saw fit" (Judges 21:25).

Second, we remember that God's silence is not the same as God's absence. In the face of injustice, Scripture gives us a Savior who does not look away. Jesus saw women fully. He listened to their pain. He defended them in public, met them in private, and restored them without shame. He welcomed the woman at the well. He refused to condemn the woman caught in adultery. He healed daughters, raised the dead at the request of sisters, and appeared first to women after the resurrection.

Jesus shows us how God thinks of women—not as property or problems, but as worthy of dignity, healing, and leadership.

Sistah, if this week's reading broke your heart—let it. You're not broken for caring. These stories should make us cry out, and in that holy cry, we find God—not in the violence, but in the refusal to ignore it.

SIT WITH IT

1. What emotions did you experience while reading the stories in Judges 11 and 19?

____

____

____

2. How might you bring those feelings honestly before God in prayer or journaling?

____

____

____

3. What does it look like for you to honor women's stories in your own faith journey?

____

____

____

BIBLE TRUTH

Judges 21:25 ends with a haunting line: "In those days Israel had no king; everyone did as they saw fit." These final words invite us to long for justice and a better way—and to seek a Savior who restores what others have ignored.

The final chapter of Judges leads directly into the opening line of Ruth. Both books are set during the same era, but they tell very different kinds of stories.

WEEK 16
THE COST OF STAYING FAITHFUL

DAILY READINGS

- ☐ Day 1: Ruth 1–4
- ☐ Day 2: 1 Samuel 1–3
- ☐ Day 3: 1 Samuel 4–7
- ☐ Day 4: 1 Samuel 8–11
- ☐ Day 5: 1 Samuel 12–14
- ☐ Day 6: 1 Samuel 15–17
- ☐ Day 7: Catch up on any readings you've missed.

THERE'S A SACRED KIND of strength that comes with keeping a vow no one else knows you made. Black women know something about that. We've been making private promises to God, to ourselves, and to those we love for generations. We make vows in waiting rooms, behind closed doors, over silent tears, and in hospital hallways. And often, those vows cost us something real.

In Ruth 2, we meet a woman who makes a vow with her life. Ruth leaves her homeland after burying her husband, choosing instead to stay with her mother-in-law, Naomi. Her commitment isn't loud, but it is radical. When Boaz sees her working in his field, he says, "May the Lord repay you for what you have done. May you be richly rewarded by the Lord, the God of Israel, under whose wings you have come to take refuge" (Ruth 2:12). Ruth's sacrifice is seen—not just by Boaz, but by God.

Then there's Hannah, a woman whose vow is born in the bitter anguish of infertility. First Samuel tells us she weeps and prays, promising to dedicate her child to God if her plea for a child is fulfilled. When her prayer is answered, she follows through in her vowed commitments: "I prayed for this child, and the Lord has granted me what I asked of him. So now I give him to the Lord" (1 Samuel 1:27–28). Her sacrifice isn't forced. It's faithful.

Both Ruth and Hannah give up something deeply personal in order to stay true to their vows with God. One leaves home. The other gives her long-awaited child. Yet, neither of their offerings are wasted.

Their stories remind us that God sees what others might miss. God receives what we give in faith. Maybe you've offered up your time, your once healthy body, your child, your dream—something costly. Maybe you're still waiting for the reward. These stories show us that even the quietest vows can echo through history.

Your sacrifice matters, even if it hurts. Even if no one claps. Even if it costs more than you thought it would. God is not indifferent to what you've laid on the altar. You are under God's wings.

Sistah, you may be walking through life holding grief in one hand and obedience in the other—but you are not alone. There is a long line of women who trusted God with what was most precious to them. And as with Ruth, with Hannah, with you—God remembers every offering.

SIT WITH IT

1. What quiet promises or vows have you made to God in this season?

2. Where have you poured from a place of lack, believing God would meet you in the gap?

3. How do you sense God acknowledging your sacrifice right now?

BIBLE TRUTH

The name "Hannah" means "grace," and Ruth is one of only five women listed in Jesus's genealogy (Matthew 1). Their sacrifices shaped history.

WEEK 17
IT WON'T BE EASY

DAILY READINGS

- Day 1: 1 Samuel 18–21
- Day 2: 1 Samuel 22–25
- Day 3: 1 Samuel 26–29
- Day 4: 1 Samuel 30–31
- Day 5: 2 Samuel 1–4
- Day 6: 2 Samuel 5–8
- Day 7: Catch up on any readings you've missed.

SOMETIMES WE THINK THAT when the hard part is over—when Saul dies, when the door opens, when the promise begins—peace will follow. Yet David's story reminds us that even in God's will, complications are par for the course. Anointing doesn't erase adversity. Destiny doesn't cancel difficulty. Even when you're walking in obedience, things can still be messy.

After years on the run—hiding in caves, surviving betrayal, grieving Saul and Jonathan's deaths—David finally stands at the edge of what God promised. The crown is near. His enemy is gone. The time has come—at least, that's how it seems.

But David doesn't rush ahead. He prays. "David inquired of the Lord. 'Shall I go up to one of the towns of Judah?' he asked. The Lord said, 'Go up.' David asked, 'Where shall I go?' 'To Hebron,' the Lord answered" (2 Samuel 2:1).

Obedience. Not ambition. That's how David moves forward.

He is anointed king—but there's a catch. He will rule over only one tribe: Judah. Although God had promised all twelve, the other eleven tribes back Saul's son, Ish-Bosheth. A civil divide begins, and David's crown comes with conflict. David must now carry the oil of his anointing while also confronting the weight of opposition. He is chosen, but not yet fully received. Appointed, but still resisted. This is the tension of walking in promise while living in process.

But don't miss this: David doesn't wait for full support from the other eleven tribes before he starts leading. Instead, he governs from Hebron for seven and a half years, trusting that what God has spoken will unfold, even if the fulfillment is delayed. And it does. By the time we reach 2 Samuel 5, the rest of Israel finally comes under his leadership, and a promise made to him as a boy is fulfilled. It takes nearly fifteen years to go from his first anointing to full kingship. That is why in 2 Samuel 6, David leads the Ark back to Jerusalem with a dance of praise that some find too bold. The promise may have seemed delayed, but it was not denied—it was delivered on time.

Sistah, if you're living in a Hebron season—where the vision is clear but the support is partial—take heart. You are still anointed. You are still appointed. The question is, how will you lead in the in-between? Will you stay faithful while the crowd is still divided? Will you walk with God when it feels like no one is walking with you? And when the breakthrough comes—will you be too refined to praise, or will you dance like David, unbothered by who is watching?

SIT WITH IT

1. Where is God asking you to obey before everything makes sense?

2. What are you doing between your 2 Samuel 2 and 2 Samuel 5 moments—between when the promise is initiated and when it begins to unfold?

3. When was the last time you praised God with your whole self, even if it felt undignified? What might be holding you back?

THIS I PRAY

God, give me the courage to lead even when I feel alone. Teach me how to trust You in the in-between—when the vision is real but the outcome is unclear. Help me to obey without full visibility, to trust You with my vulnerability, and to praise without shame when I stand in the victory. Let my life echo David's: faithful, patient, and free. In Jesus's name, Amen.

WEEK 18

YOUR SEAT AT THE TABLE

DAILY READINGS

- Day 1: 2 Samuel 9–12
- Day 2: 2 Samuel 13–15
- Day 3: 2 Samuel 16–18
- Day 4: 2 Samuel 19–21
- Day 5: 2 Samuel 22–24
- Day 6: Psalms 38–41
- Day 7: Catch up on any readings you've missed.

SOME PAIN ISN'T SELF-INFLICTED—it's inherited. Some damage we carry didn't come from a poor choice, but from being dropped. Mephibosheth's story begins with royalty and yet he eventually finds himself in exile. The grandson of Saul and son of Jonathan, Mephibosheth was born into a promise. But when tragedy struck, his nurse dropped him while fleeing danger. "Jonathan son of Saul had a son who was lame in both feet. He was five years old when...his nurse picked him up and fled, but as she hurried to leave, he fell and became disabled" (2 Samuel 4:4).

By 2 Samuel 9, Mephibosheth is living in Lo Debar—a place known for having no communication and no hope. Lo Debar is a place where people go when they've been dropped, discarded, or disqualified. Yet David, honoring his covenant with Jonathan, sends for Mephibosheth—not to punish him, but to restore him. "'Don't be afraid,' David said to him, 'for I will surely show you kindness...I will restore to you all the land that belonged to your grandfather Saul, and you will always eat at my table'" (2 Samuel 9:7).

David doesn't erase Mephibosheth's limp. Instead, he covers it with kindness. At the king's table, no one can see what made him feel unworthy. His place is secured not by perfection, but by promise. No drop, no diagnosis, no decision beyond his control could prevent him from finding his rightful place in the palace.

Mephibosheth isn't the only one whose story is reshaped. The text says he was living with a man named Makir, a caretaker. Perhaps he, too, had dreams that were deferred by the call to care for someone else—responsibilities he didn't choose. He represents those of us who carry others. Those whose lives are shaped by someone else's needs. As a single mother raising a son who learns differently, I carry this reality in my own bones. I know the tension of honoring someone's dignity but also acknowledging the weight of responsibility.

Many of us live at the same intersection. We've been wounded, and we're carrying other: the parent who failed us, the sibling who depends on us, the child whose needs never end, and the system that may not see us. We are living in Lo Debar, and we are tired.

Sis, here is the hope: Lo Debar is not your final destination. It may describe your surroundings, but it doesn't define your destiny. The pain is real, but so is the call to come out of that place. There is still a seat for you at the table. By the time grace reaches you, the table will already be set—covering the pain while crowning the survivor in you.

SIT WITH IT

1. Where in your life have you carried the weight of someone else's decision? Can you name it honestly?

2. What parts of your story feel beyond healing right now?

3. Who are you carrying that God may also be calling to the table?

BIBLE TRUTH

"Lo Debar" means "no pasture" or "no word." It was a desolate, barren place—both physically and symbolically. Mephibosheth was living in a space of silence and lack when grace came looking for him.

WEEK 19

DON'T QUIT

DAILY READINGS

- Day 1: 1 Kings 1–4
- Day 2: 1 Kings 5–7
- Day 3: 1 Kings 8–10
- Day 4: 1 Kings 11–14
- Day 5: 1 Kings 15–18
- Day 6: 1 Kings 19–22
- Day 7: Catch up on any readings you've missed.

DURING A SEASON OF drought, when famine has emptied the land and fear is palpably in the air, God directs Elijah to a woman on the brink.

This is soon after Elijah's first public assignment. He comes on the scene boldly, declaring that rain will stop until he says otherwise. Then he disappears into hiding, sustained by a brook and birds. But when even that brook dries up, God sends him to Zarephath with instructions to meet a widow. "Go at once to Zarephath... I have directed a widow there to supply you with food" (1 Kings 17:9).

Her pantry is almost bare. Her heart, nearly broken. She's down to her last meal and a handful of hope. She's not preparing to serve—she's preparing to die.

Still, Elijah makes a bold ask: "Don't be afraid. Go home and do as you have said. But first make a small loaf of bread for me... For this is what the Lord, the God of Israel, says: 'The jar of flour will not be used up and the jug of oil will not run dry'" (1 Kings 17:13–14).

She has every reason to say no. But instead, she believes—just enough—to act. And that little bit of faith stretches into a miracle that sustains her household day after day.

By the time we reach 1 Kings 19, after confronting hundreds of false prophets and calling down fire from heaven, Elijah runs. He crashes. He is experiencing burnout. He goes so far as to ask God to take his life. Like the widow in Zarephath, even prophets want to quit. Even the ones God uses might end up under a broom tree, too tired to keep going.

God sees exhaustion, and God supplies sustenance and strength. Sometimes it's oil in a jar. Sometimes it's fire from heaven. Sometimes it's sleep and a snack. Sometimes it's a gentle breeze. But I know for sure that God meets our breaking point with deep care each and every time.

So don't quit. Not yet. If you've been living in survival mode, if you're preparing to throw in the towel, if you've convinced yourself the story is over—pause. You might just be one act of courage away from a miracle that carries you forward.

Sistah, obedience doesn't mean you won't feel physical, mental, emotional, and even spiritual exhaustion. It means you believe there's still something worth showing up for. You don't need a full plan—just enough trust to take the next step. God will meet you there.

SIT WITH IT

1. What's one place in your life where you feel like giving up? What would it take to keep going one more day?

2. Where might God be inviting you to act in faith, even if it feels risky or premature?

3. When have you experienced burnout? What surprised you about how God met you there?

SIS, TRY THIS

Choose one small act of faith this week—especially in a place where you feel tired, stretched, or unsure. Write down what it costs you to say yes anyway. Then return to that list in prayer and ask God to multiply what feels like barely enough.

WEEK 20

WHEN THE MANTLE FALLS AND THE EDGE SLIPS

DAILY READINGS

- Day 1: 2 Kings 1–3
- Day 2: 2 Kings 4–7
- Day 3: 2 Kings 8–11
- Day 4: 2 Kings 12–15
- Day 5: 2 Kings 16–18
- Day 6: 2 Kings 19–22
- Day 7: Catch up on any readings you've missed.

"'LET ME INHERIT A double portion of your spirit,' Elisha replied. 'You have asked a difficult thing,' Elijah said, 'yet if you see me when I am taken from you, it will be yours'" (2 Kings 2:9–10). This moment is both sacred and sorrowful. Elisha is watching his mentor, Elijah, prepare for departure. He's been faithful, loyal, and patient. And now, he's bold enough to ask for a double portion—not of Elijah's fame, but of his spirit. That request is granted the moment Elijah is swept away and Elisha is left holding the mantle.

What is the mantle? In the ancient Near East, a prophet's mantle was a cloak, often made of animal skin, worn as a sign of divine calling. It represented spiritual authority, responsibility, and anointing. When Elijah's mantle falls, it's more than fabric—it's the sacred transfer of prophetic trust. Elisha picks it up with trembling hands and torn clothes.

Sometimes the call comes with grief. Sometimes receiving what's next means releasing who came before.

But even after the new mantle parts the waters and the miracles begin, Elisha's story reminds us the anointed can still lose their edge.

In 2 Kings 6, a prophet-in-training is chopping wood when the iron axe-head flies off and sinks into the water below. Panicked, he cries out, "It was borrowed!" (2 Kings 6:5). Iron was rare and costly; this wasn't just a tool, it was a trust. Elisha doesn't shame him at his request for help. He asks, "Where did it fall?" (2 Kings 6:6). Only when the prophet-in-training points to where it fell does the act of recovery begin.

There will be seasons when you carry the mantle with boldness—and others when fatigue or fear dulls your clarity. The best of us have misplaced what was entrusted to us: our vision, our confidence, our spiritual edge. But I am a living witness that you can get it back.

Sistah, ask God to help you name the moment—the moment when it fell together and the moment when it fell apart. Ask God to lead you to a trusted space where you can safely share where it fell. When healing begins in honesty, restoration is always possible.

This is the rhythm of life. The same Elisha who caught the mantle became the mentor who helped others recover what they lost. You owe it to yourself to discover who you are on both sides of what fell.

SIT WITH IT

1. What mantle—or sense of purpose—has God passed to you through someone else's life or legacy?

2. Can you name where something in your life "fell apart"? What would it look like to point to that place honestly?

3. Where is God inviting you to recover what was lost, and who might be a trusted voice to walk with you?

THIS I PRAY

God, I thank You for every person who helped me become who I am. Thank You for the mantles I've received—some handed down with joy, others through grief. When I lose my edge, show me where it fell. Give me courage to ask, wisdom to trust, and faith to believe it's not too late. In Jesus's name, amen.

WEEK 21
NEIGHBOR IS A VERB

DAILY READINGS

- [ ] Day 1: 2 Kings 23–25
- [ ] Day 2: Luke 1–4
- [ ] Day 3: Luke 5–7
- [ ] Day 4: Luke 8–11
- [ ] Day 5: Luke 12–14
- [ ] Day 6: Luke 15–18
- [ ] Day 7: Catch up on any readings you've missed.

I ONCE HAD A seminary professor say, "In Luke's Gospel, Jesus spends more time at dinner parties than in the temple." That observation has stayed with me. This Gospel is different. Where Matthew leans into Jewish lineage and Mark moves fast through miracles, Luke slows down to elevate the margins. His is a Gospel of table fellowship, reversed expectations, and wide-open grace.

So when we arrive at Luke 10:25–37, the setup matters.

A lawyer stands up—not to learn, but to trap. He asks, "What must I do to inherit eternal life?" (Luke 10:25). Jesus responds with a question of his own, and the man answers: "Love God and love your neighbor." But then, "wanting to justify himself," he asks: "And who is my neighbor?" (Luke 10:29).

This is not a question of compassion; it's a question of control. Who is in, and who is out? He is ultimately asking: *Who can be loved without crossing a line?*

Jesus answers with a story. A man is attacked and left for dead. A priest passes. A Levite passes. These are respected religious figures—leaders with titles and temple assignments. But they choose destination over deliverance, religious codes over righteous compassion, and purity over proximity.

Then comes a Samaritan. This isn't just unexpected; it's an offensive plot twist for his listeners. There were rules at play here because Jews and Samaritans didn't associate. There was a history of deep division. So for Jesus to cast a Samaritan as the hero of this parable is hard for the crowd to hear. But that's the point. God's love moves through unexpected people.

And not only does the Samaritan stop to help the man left behind by religious leaders—he tends wounds, pays expenses, and promises follow-up care. He doesn't just pass by with thoughts and prayers. He acts. He gets close despite the rules. He becomes a neighbor through his actions.

Jesus ends the story not by asking, "Which man was the most like you?" but, "Which of these three do you think was a neighbor?"

(Luke 10:36). The man replies, "The one who had mercy on him." Jesus simply says: "Go and do likewise" (Luke 10:37).

My sister, Jesus isn't asking who your neighbor is. He's asking whether you're being neighborly to everyone you meet. Mercy, not status. Proximity, not comfort. Neighbor is not a label to wear—it's a life to live.

SIT WITH IT

1. Have you ever chosen comfort, convenience, or religious rules over compassion?

   ____

   ____

   ____

2. Who have you been hesitant to see as my neighbor—and why?

   ____

   ____

   ____

3. What would it look like to live out mercy as a daily practice, not just a belief?

   ____

   ____

   ____

BIBLE TRUTH

According to Jewish purity laws, touching blood or a wounded body could make someone ritually "unclean." The priest and Levite may have avoided the injured man to stay pure. But Jesus redefines righteousness: Love is greater than law, and compassion is always holy.

WEEK 22

LAMENT THAT WON'T LET GO

DAILY READINGS

- ☐ Day 1: Luke 19–21
- ☐ Day 2: Luke 22–24
- ☐ Day 3: Psalms 42–47
- ☐ Day 4: Psalms 48–54
- ☐ Day 5: Psalms 55–61
- ☐ Day 6: Psalms 62–67
- ☐ Day 7: Catch up on any readings you've missed.

PSALM 42 MARKS A shift in the book of Psalms. It opens Book II (Psalms 42–72), moving from personal prayers toward communal longing. This Psalm is linked to the sons of Korah, Levitical temple singers descended from Korah himself. Though Korah rebelled against Moses and was judged by God (Numbers 16), his descendants became worship leaders. That's the beauty of grace—God transforms failure into praise and gives new purpose to a broken legacy.

We hear the ache immediately: "As the deer pants for streams of water, so my soul pants for you, my God" (Psalm 42:1). It's not poetic—it's desperate. The psalmist is worn out, cut off from sacred space, and aching for God. Then comes a self-directed plea: "Why, my soul, are you downcast?... Put your hope in God, for I will yet praise Him" (Psalm 42:5).

That "yet" is everything.

I've sat with women in my church who praised through tears, who kept singing when God felt silent. I've been one of them myself. Psalm 42 doesn't offer resolution. But it gives us rhythm—grief and memory, sorrow and hope. You don't have to resolve your pain to be faithful. Just stay in the conversation. Lament is a holy language too.

We've seen this as a people. In 2015, nine Black worshippers were murdered during Bible study at Emanuel AME Church in Charleston, South Carolina. The sorrow was deep. But the return to worship was deeper. That wasn't performance. It was protest and praise, offered in the same breath. That was lament with backbone.

And Jesus? He lamented too. In Luke 22, he prays in Gethsemane, sweating like drops of blood as he prepares to carry the weight of the world. Then in Luke 24, two disciples walk the road to Emmaus, saying, "We had hoped..." (Luke 24:21). Disappointed and disoriented, they don't recognize Jesus walking beside them. As he teaches, their hearts begin to burn. And when he breaks bread, they finally see: He has been with them in their lament all along.

Sistah, if your soul is tired, you're not alone. You don't have to fake your praise. Lament is how we hold space for sorrow without letting it swallow our faith. It's how we love God without pretending. It is sacred. It is scriptural. And it is strong. Lament doesn't silence your worship—it strengthens it.

Lament isn't weakness—it's worship with backbone.

SIT WITH IT

1. Where in your life are you saying, "I had hoped"? How might God still be walking beside you in that disappointment?

2. What's one moment of grief you've been afraid to name out loud?

3. How have you been taught to perform strength instead of practicing lament? What would honest worship look like for you right now?

SIS, TRY THIS

1. Take ten minutes this week to write a "yet" prayer. Tell God the truth—your weariness, your ache, your waiting.
2. Then, end the prayer with one line of defiant hope. It can be simple: "Yet I will trust You." "Yet I believe You are near." Let lament and hope share the same page.

WEEK 23

HOW TO PRAY A BODACIOUS PRAYER

DAILY READINGS

- Day 1: 1 Chronicles 1–4
- Day 2: 1 Chronicles 5–8
- Day 3: 1 Chronicles 9–12
- Day 4: 1 Chronicles 13–16
- Day 5: 1 Chronicles 17–19
- Day 6: 1 Chronicles 20–22
- Day 7: Catch up on any readings you've missed.

BURIED INSIDE A LONG list of genealogies—chapter after chapter of who begat whom—comes a sudden disruption. A pause in the rhythm. A breath of boldness.

"Jabez cried out to the God of Israel, 'Oh, that you would bless me and enlarge my territory! Let your hand be with me, and keep me from harm so that I will be free from pain.' And God granted his request." (1 Chronicles 4:10)

That's it. No origin story, no miracles, no descendants. Just a name that means "pain"—and a prayer that defies it.

In the ancient world, names carried prophetic weight. To be called "Jabez" was to walk through life shaped by sorrow. But instead of accepting that identity, Jabez interrupted the narrative. He didn't ask God to erase the past—he asked God to enlarge his future. He asked for blessing, for presence, for protection, for freedom.

And God said yes.

Sistah, I've learned something in my own journey: We often limit God because of what we've survived. We pray safe prayers. Small prayers. Scarcity prayers. But Jabez shows us another way. Not long ago, I started praying, "God, show me how good it can get." And something shifted. That prayer didn't set terms or conditions—it simply made room. It didn't restrict God; it released God. It was trust. It was hunger. It was holy curiosity. It was bold faith. And God responded.

I think of Sojourner Truth—a formerly enslaved woman who, in 1828, prayed bold prayers and marched into a courtroom to demand her son's freedom. It had never been done before. But she believed in a God who could override man-made limits. And she won. Her prayer didn't just shift her pain—it shifted the law. That's the power of bodacious faith. It moves heaven. It disrupts history. It creates possibility where there was none.

When we pray bodacious prayers, we shift things. We shift *moments*—unlocking divine timing. We shift *movements*—praying freedom into families, congregations, and communities. And we shift those who *minister*—including ourselves. Jabez was not a priest or prophet. He was just one person who dared to ask for more.

You don't need a platform. You don't need a perfect record. You don't need a long speech. Just one sentence, offered in faith, can reroute the trajectory of your life.

Ask boldly. Pray expansively. Refuse to let pain define your praise.

God is still honoring bodacious prayers.

SIT WITH IT

1. Have you been praying in a way that protects you from disappointment, or opens you to divine possibility?

2. Where have you accepted pain as permanent when God may be inviting you to ask for something better?

3. What would your prayer sound like if you truly believed God wanted to say yes?

VERSE OF THE WEEK

Jabez cried out to the God of Israel, "Oh, that you would bless me and enlarge my territory! Let your hand be with me, and keep me from harm so that I will be free from pain." And God granted his request.

1 Chronicles 4:10

WEEK 24

GLORY ISN'T THE GOAL

DAILY READINGS

- Day 1: 1 Chronicles 23–26
- Day 2: 1 Chronicles 27–29
- Day 3: 2 Chronicles 1–3
- Day 4: 2 Chronicles 4–7
- Day 5: 2 Chronicles 8–10
- Day 6: 2 Chronicles 11–13
- Day 7: Catch up on any readings you've missed.

BY THE TIME WE reach 1 Chronicles 28, David is old, tender, and nearing the end. He once dreamed of building the temple himself—but God said no. David could have clung to control. Instead, he releases the vision, entrusts the next generation, and gives generously from what he has. "Be strong and courageous, and do the work," he tells Solomon. "Do not be afraid or discouraged, for the Lord God, my God, is with you" (1 Chronicles 28:20).

It's one thing to dream. It's another to accept that your dream will outlive you, and still bless it anyway. That's spiritual maturity. David doesn't need to finish the temple to affirm its holiness. He trusts God. He equips Solomon with more than he received. That's legacy. David models a leadership handoff that centers on wisdom, community, and clarity—not ego or fear, which Saul had with him.

And when the time comes—when the Ark is placed and the people sing—Scripture says, "Then the temple of the Lord was filled with the cloud, and the priests could not perform their service because of the cloud, for the glory of the Lord filled the temple of God" (2 Chronicles 5:13–14). You will notice the glory doesn't come at the moment of completion, but as a response to worship, sacrifice, and obedience. This cloud, this glory, is what we refer to as a "theophany"—a visible manifestation of divine presence—echoing the same holy encounter we read about in Exodus 40:34 when God filled the tabernacle.

Black women know this rhythm well. We plant seeds—maybe even get to water them—but we don't always live to see them bloom. In countless Black churches, women prepare the communion table but are not invited to serve it. We lead choirs, raise funds, teach Sunday School, and hold families and congregations together—yet often remain behind the curtain when the celebration comes. Still, let us name this work as holy.

A sacred space is not made sacred by grandeur. Not by gold or gowns or who holds the mic. A space becomes sacred—a sanctuary, if you will—when God inhabits it. And sometimes, what makes room for that presence isn't visibility—it's quiet obedience. Unseen labor. Open hands. The holiness is in the preparation. In the offering. In the trust that what we start, God will finish.

Sistah, maybe you're the one holding blueprints no one else sees. Maybe your offering is preparation, not completion. That doesn't make your contribution any less sacred. Don't underestimate the holiness of what you're building. God fills what we prepare by faith.

SIT WITH IT

1. Where in your life are you being asked to hand something off or release control? What emotions come up as you consider letting go of the outcome?

____

____

____

2. Can you name a place where your quiet preparation made space for someone else's breakthrough? How did that experience shape your understanding of legacy?

____

____

____

3. What does it mean for you, in this season, to believe that unseen labor is still sacred? Where are you trusting God to fill what you've faithfully prepared?

BIBLE TRUTH

The Queen of Sheba (2 Chronicles 9) was a powerful woman of color who brought hard questions and generous gifts to Solomon. She wasn't just curious—she was discerning. Her story affirms that wisdom, wealth, and spiritual authority have long belonged to Black women.

WEEK 25

A WISE WOMAN BUILDS

DAILY READINGS

- Day 1: Proverbs 18–21
- Day 2: Proverbs 22–24
- Day 3: Proverbs 25–27
- Day 4: Proverbs 28–31
- Day 5: 2 Chronicles 14–16
- Day 6: 2 Chronicles 17–19
- Day 7: Catch up on any readings you've missed.

THE VIRTUOUS WOMAN OF Proverbs 31 is familiar to many—a text we've heard quoted from pulpits and women's conferences for generations. But what's often missed is that these words aren't a man describing a woman. They are the teachings of a mother—a queen, in fact—offering wisdom to her son. Before she ever talks about a virtuous woman, she warns him not to misuse his power or ignore injustice. Then she says, essentially, *Watch for this*. Watch for the kind of woman who leads with wisdom and lives with purpose.

The woman she describes is not an ideal to mimic. She is a multidimensional force. She trades, teaches, protects, prays, invests, leads, and laughs. She doesn't just run a household—she sustains a community. And she does it not for applause, but from a place of deep purpose. This isn't a checklist to measure your worth. It's a celebration of what wisdom can do when it flows through a woman fully rooted in her God and in herself. Not every woman will do all these things, but every woman has the right to be seen as whole.

The wisdom personified throughout Proverbs, and exemplified in chapter 31, also shapes the reign of Jehoshaphat. He sees God and makes mistakes but course-corrects after his failed alliance with Ahab. Then he appoints judges who lead with integrity: "Consider carefully what you do, because you are not judging for mere mortals but for the Lord...Judge carefully, for with the Lord our God there is no injustice or partiality or bribery" (2 Chronicles 19:6–7).

Wisdom looks like that—knowing not only what to do, but also how to navigate the challenges of life. I think of Jarena Lee, the first woman authorized to preach in the African Methodist Episcopal Church. She knew the call of God in her bones, but the church refused her at first. Still, she spoke wherever she could—pulpits, fields, homes. She didn't wait for permission. She pressed forward in faith. Eventually, the same church that once silenced her could no longer deny her wisdom or her witness. That's what navigating adversity looks like when you know what God put in you is too powerful to waste.

Sistah, you don't have to be all things to all people to be worthy. You don't have to perform strength to prove value. Wisdom doesn't mean you get everything right; it means you move with purpose, you pivot with grace, and you protect what matters. Whatever you're building, let it be shaped by wisdom, not pressure. And let that wisdom make you free.

SIT WITH IT

1. In what areas of your life are you being invited to lead with wisdom—not perfection, not performance, but grounded wisdom?

2. How has the traditional teaching of the virtuous woman in Proverbs 31 shaped how you see yourself? What parts of that image need to be reclaimed, released, or reimagined?

3. Can you name a moment when you walked away from something that no longer honored your calling? What did that require of you?

VERSE OF THE WEEK

She speaks with wisdom, and faithful instruction is on her tongue.

Proverbs 31:26

WEEK 26

WHEN THE PEOPLE RETURN

DAILY READINGS

- Day 1: 2 Chronicles 20–24
- Day 2: 2 Chronicles 25–28
- Day 3: 2 Chronicles 29–32
- Day 4: 2 Chronicles 33–36
- Day 5: Psalms 68–72
- Day 6: Psalms 73–78
- Day 7: Catch up on any readings you've missed.

BY THE TIME HEZEKIAH becomes king of Judah, the temple is shut. His father, Ahaz, desecrated the sacred space—closing the doors, silencing worship, and replacing God's altar with foreign idols (2 Chronicles 28:24). But in the very first month of his reign, Hezekiah does something remarkable: "He opened the doors of the temple of the Lord and repaired them" (2 Chronicles 29:3). He doesn't start with politics or public works—he starts with worship.

He calls the priests, purifies the temple, and reinstates sacred song. But he doesn't stop there. In chapters 30 and 31, he sends messengers across Israel and Judah, inviting the people to return. Some mock the invitation. Others weep. Still, a remnant comes. And when they do, they don't just reopen the building—they revive the community. Worship returns. Fellowship deepens. God shows up.

Hezekiah's reforms are more than a leadership strategy—they're a sacred reversal of generational harm. He doesn't treat revival as a moment, but as a sustained process: purification, reeducation, reconnection. His commitment reshapes not just religious practice, but also communal identity. Psalm 78 mirrors this with poetic honesty. It names the people's rebellion, but exalts God's mercy: "Yet he was merciful; he forgave their iniquities...Time after time he restrained his anger" (Psalm 78:38). When we forget God, God still remembers us.

I've lived this. The church that eventually called me to serve as senior pastor had experienced devastating loss: Its entire edifice, including the sanctuary, was destroyed by fire. The doors remained shut. But the Spirit never left. When we began to gather again—first among ashes, then through holy imagination—it wasn't about bricks or budgets. It was about kindling worship, restoring kinship, and reimagining sacred community.

That's what Hezekiah models: a revival rooted in presence, not performance. Revival reorients us. It breaks old cycles. It reminds us that sacred spaces—both physical and spiritual—can be healed and inhabited again. And it tells the truth: God doesn't wait for perfection to return. God comes when we open the door.

Sistah, maybe something sacred in your life has been shut down for a while. Maybe the fire came. The people scattered. The songs stopped. But God hasn't gone anywhere. Revival doesn't always look like shouting—it can begin with an open door, a repaired altar, a willingness to try again. So go on. Start with worship. Let God do the rest.

SIT WITH IT

1. What sacred doors in your life have been closed—and what might it look like to open them again?

2. How do you define revival in your own story? Where do you long for it now?

3. In what ways has God remembered you—even when you forgot your way?

SIS, TRY THIS

1. This week, light a candle or play a worship song that once brought you peace. Let the flame or the music mark this time as intentional—no rushing, no multitasking, just space to be present.

2. As the candle burns or the song plays, write a prayer of return, naming what sacred part of your life you want to reopen.

3. Don't worry about getting the words right or making the prayer sound polished. This isn't about perfection. It's about choosing to begin again, right where you are.

WEEK 27

FOR SUCH A TIME AS THIS

DAILY READINGS

- ☐ Day 1: Esther 1–3
- ☐ Day 2: Esther 4–6
- ☐ Day 3: Esther 7–10
- ☐ Day 4: Psalms 79–84
- ☐ Day 5: Psalms 85–89
- ☐ Day 6: Psalms 90–96
- ☐ Day 7: Catch up on any readings you've missed.

WHAT DO YOU THINK of when you think of courage?

Esther's story reminds us that courage doesn't always start loud. Sometimes it begins as a whisper in your spirit, a stirring you can't ignore. The Spirit prepares us, positions us, and then nudges us toward purpose. The courage to show up—even when it's costly—is part of our spiritual inheritance as Black women.

Esther's tale unfolds in the shadows of empire. She's a Jewish woman living in exile, taken into the palace after Queen Vashti is banished for refusing to come when the king called—wearing her royal crown and *nothing else*. Esther doesn't rise by romance. She's chosen for her beauty, not her brilliance. She's placed in a role that hides her identity, surrounded by systems never meant for her to thrive.

And still, God is moving—quietly, faithfully—beneath the surface.

The crisis comes when Haman, a powerful official, convinces the king to sign off on genocide. Mordecai, Esther's cousin, urges her to intervene. At first, she's afraid—and for good reason. Approaching the king without invitation could cost her life. But Mordecai says, "And who knows but that you have come to your royal position for such a time as this?" (Esther 4:14).

Esther doesn't rush. She calls for a fast. She listens. She plans. She gathers her people before risking everything. And when the time is right, she speaks. Her voice doesn't just save lives; it also revives hope.

This story isn't just about bravery. It's also about wisdom, timing, and collective survival. Esther doesn't chase the spotlight—she uses it. Her courage is both private and public, both silent and strategic. And though God's name never appears in the book, divine presence pulses through every risk. It's Spirit-led strategy, shaped in sacred silence.

Psalm 85:6 says, "Will you not revive us again, that your people may rejoice in you?" That's what Esther makes space for—a revival of joy, justice, and generational safety. She becomes a mirror for every woman who's ever wondered if her moment has come.

Sistah, maybe you've been asking, *Why am I here*? Or feeling the urge to speak up, though staying quiet feels safer. Don't miss this: You're not in the wrong room. You're not too early or too late. You might be where you are for *exactly such a time as this*. You don't have to say everything. But when it's time to speak—do it with courage. When it's time to move—do it with wisdom. And trust God will meet you in the risk.

SIT WITH IT

1. What fears or insecurities have kept you silent in rooms where your voice was needed?

2. Have you ever felt called to act "for such a time as this"? What did it cost you, and what did it grow in you?

3. How do you discern when it's time to speak, wait, or prepare in sacred silence?

THIS I PRAY

God who positions us with purpose, Thank You for moving even when I can't see You. When I feel unqualified or afraid, remind me that You are not waiting on my perfection—You're inviting my yes. Give me wisdom to wait, boldness to speak, and clarity to know when to do each. Let my courage serve not just myself, but also those who are counting on me to show up. May I trust that where You place me, You will also prepare me. And when the time comes, let me rise—for such a time as this. In Jesus's name, amen.

WEEK 28

WHEN THE ANSWERS DON'T HELP

DAILY READINGS

- Day 1: Job 1–3
- Day 2: Job 4–7
- Day 3: Job 8–11
- Day 4: Job 12–14
- Day 5: Job 15–17
- Day 6: Job 18–21
- Day 7: Catch up on any readings you've missed.

THE BOOK OF JOB is wisdom literature that wrestles with a timeless question: Why do the righteous suffer? It invites us into a poetic, often painful dialogue between human anguish and divine silence. Job's story is less about answers and more about staying faithful when life stops making sense.

It all starts with a conversation we were never meant to overhear: In the courts of heaven, an accuser challenges Job's integrity, and God allows Job's faith to be tested.

In Job 1:8, God points out that Job is faithful, blameless, a man of deep integrity—and that's what makes him a target. Not sin. Not rebellion. Devotion. His suffering isn't punishment—it comes because heaven permits his faith to be tested.

What unfolds is a cosmic wager with earthly consequences. Job loses everything—his children, his home, his health. And just when the silence of grief settles in, his friends show up. At first, they sit with him in sacred stillness. But soon, their words cut like knives. They imply he must have done something to deserve this. They don't just misunderstand Job—they misrepresent God.

Job responds, "Anyone who withholds kindness from a friend forsakes the fear of the Almighty" (Job 6:14). In other words: You can't claim to fear God while wounding the already wounded. Job doesn't curse God, but he does cry out. Loudly. Honestly. His sorrow is not sanitized. And still, God calls him faithful.

That tension between divine favor and devastating loss is familiar to many Black women. We are often the most faithful and the most afflicted. We give, pray, fast, show up—and still face unbearable pain. Then, like Job, we're told to "trust God," as if faith means silence. As if real believers don't scream into the night.

Sis, have you ever felt singled out by God and then abandoned? Have friends tried to "explain" your pain instead of sitting in it with you? Job's story tells the truth: Sometimes the strongest thing you can do is not have answers—but hold on anyway.

You don't have to prove your innocence or justify your tears. You are not suffering because you failed. You might be suffering because you're seen. And yes—it hurts. But even in the ache, you are not alone. God is still paying attention. And God can handle your honesty. Your lament is not weakness; it's faith that refuses to quit.

SIT WITH IT

1. When have you felt most misunderstood in your suffering? What would it have meant for someone to simply sit with you?

2. What kind of friend are you to others in their pain? Are you offering presence, or pressuring them to make sense of what can't be explained?

3. Do you believe God can handle your honesty, your anger, your doubt? Why or why not?

SIS, TRY THIS

This week, write out your own uncensored lament to God. Name the ache, the questions, even the anger. Then, instead of rushing to fix it, sit in silence for five minutes and let your honesty itself become prayer.

WEEK 29

NOW I SEE

DAILY READINGS

- Day 1: Job 22–24
- Day 2: Job 25–28
- Day 3: Job 29–31
- Day 4: Job 32–35
- Day 5: Job 36–39
- Day 6: Job 40–42
- Day 7: Catch up on any readings you've missed.

BY THE TIME WE reach the end of Job, we've seen him lose almost everything: his children, his health, his livelihood, his sense of justice. We've heard the long and often painful advice of his friends, who try to explain God but never truly listen to Job's heart. We've watched him wrestle aloud—angry, honest, searching, desperate for an audience with the Almighty. Finally, in chapter 38, God answers—not with explanations, but with presence.

In Job 42:5, Job utters a quiet confession: "My ears had heard of you, but now my eyes have seen you."

It's a shift. A sacred awakening. What Job once knew through secondhand stories, he now knows through lived experience. God is no longer just an idea or a doctrine. God has become real—personal.

That's the arc of spiritual maturity, isn't it? Many of us grew up hearing about God from elders who prayed in ways we didn't yet understand. As children, we might have chuckled when someone said, "Trouble don't last always," or, "The Lord has been better to me than I've been to myself." But after life happens—after heartbreak, loss, and waiting—we start saying those same things. Because now we've seen God for ourselves.

It reminds me of the old hymn "Amazing Grace," written by John Newton, a former slave trader who turned to faith after surviving a violent storm at sea. That night began a long, painful journey of repentance and reformation. His words ring true across generations:

Amazing grace! How sweet the sound,
That saved a wretch like me!
I once was lost, but now am found,
Was blind, but now I see.

Like Job, Newton came to know God not just in theory, but through encounter. Through grief. Through grace.

Sis, sometimes it takes suffering to see clearly. That doesn't mean God caused the pain—but it does mean that even in our hardest seasons, God shows up. The blessing isn't just in the restoration. There is always a blessing in the revelation—those moments when God is known to us in new ways. The revelation may not answer every question, but it deepens our relationship. We've felt the nearness in the valley. We've heard God's voice in the storm. We've cried out—and been met, not always with answers, but with presence.

So if you're in a season of suffering, keep going. What you're learning about God now will carry you later. And one day, someone will ask how you kept the faith—and you'll say, "Sis, I see now. I didn't always understand it, but God was with me all along."

SIT WITH IT

1. What's something you used to hear about God that you now understand more deeply through your own experience?

2. Where have you seen God more clearly—not because your pain disappeared, but because God showed up in it?

3. Who are the "church mothers" or spiritual elders whose faith shaped you? How have you grown into the truths they used to say?

VERSE OF THE WEEK

"My ears had heard of you, but now my eyes have seen you."

Job 42:5

WEEK 30

A CAREGIVER'S CROSSROADS

DAILY READINGS

- Day 1: John 1–4
- Day 2: John 5–8
- Day 3: John 9–11
- Day 4: John 12–15
- Day 5: John 16–18
- Day 6: John 19–21
- Day 7: Catch up on any readings you've missed.

JOHN'S GOSPEL DOESN'T OPEN with a manger or a genealogy. It begins with eternity: "In the beginning was the Word" (John 1:1). Where Matthew, Mark, and Luke walk us through the earthly life of Jesus, John lifts the veil. He gives us mystery and majesty, signs and glory. His Gospel is the most intimate—filled with long conversations, quiet miracles, and deeply personal moments not found anywhere else. And when we reach the cross, John shows us something no other Gospel does: a sacred caregiving exchange in Jesus's final breaths.

Jesus—beaten, bleeding, gasping for air—looks down and sees His mother standing near the cross. Next to her is the beloved disciple, likely John himself. And in this excruciating moment, Jesus tells his mother, "Woman, here is your son," and the disciple, "Here is your mother" (John 19:26–27). Even in agony, Jesus is arranging care, making provision, and building community.

This moment is drenched in responsibility. Jesus is the oldest son. Joseph is gone, and with Jesus's impending death, Mary's well-being is suddenly uncertain. According to custom, her other sons—James, Joseph, Simon, and Judas—should have stepped in to provide her care. But they are missing. And that absence isn't just logistical—it's emotional. The people who should have held her up have left a void. The responsibility falls on someone else. And Jesus, even while dying, fills the gap.

John, too, is impacted. He doesn't just become a caretaker for a non-blood relative—he becomes family. In a single sentence, Jesus rewrites John's assignment and reframes his identity. He is no longer just a disciple; he is now a son. A provider. A steady presence in someone else's storm. Perhaps that's why Jesus chooses him—not because of biology, but because of presence. Because John stays.

Jesus doesn't leave Mary without care and protection. He doesn't leave John without grace. In this holy exchange, He redefines family and shows us how sacred responsibility is often forged in the fire of suffering.

Sis, maybe you're standing at your own caregiving crossroads—doing more than you were asked, carrying more than you thought possible, giving more than you receive. And still, you keep showing up. You hold people together. You make sure someone eats, sleeps, and survives. And sometimes, you wonder: *Who's holding me?*

Here's the truth: The same Jesus who made sure His mother was covered is covering you. The same God who entrusted John with an unexpected assignment is giving you grace for your own. When God calls you to carry something, God also surrounds you—sometimes with sacred community and other times with strength you didn't know you had.

You may feel stretched, overlooked, or alone, but God sees you. And there will always be enough for the assignment.

SIT WITH IT

1. What surprised you most about the Gospel of John compared to the other Gospels? How did it deepen your understanding of who Jesus is?

2. What caregiving responsibilities are you carrying right now? Where do you need help, strength, or the freedom to let go?

3. Have you ever stepped into a caregiving role you didn't expect? What did it teach you about love, limits, or community?

THIS I PRAY

God who sees and provides, You know the weight I carry and the weariness I sometimes hide. Give me grace for what I've been asked to carry—especially when it feels like too much. Remind me I am not alone. Surround me with sacred community. Help me release resentment and receive help. Let me serve with love, not obligation, and rest with trust, not guilt. You entrusted me with this role, so I trust You'll also sustain me through it. In Jesus's name, amen.

WEEK 31

THE SACREDNESS OF ORDINARY JOY

DAILY READINGS

- Day 1: Ecclesiastes 1–4
- Day 2: Ecclesiastes 5–8
- Day 3: Ecclesiastes 9–12
- Day 4: Psalms 97–100
- Day 5: Psalms 101–103
- Day 6: Psalms 104–106
- Day 7: Catch up on any readings you've missed.

FOR BLACK WOMEN WHO'VE had to hold complexity without guaranteed resolution, Ecclesiastes may feel like a familiar companion. This is not the voice of a naive theologian—it's the well-worn wisdom of someone who has survived systems, seen injustice, and still found ways to keep going. In Ecclesiastes 4:1, the writer laments that the tears of the oppressed "have no comforter." Yet instead of shutting down, "the Teacher" who wrote this book leans in, looking for meaning not in power or performance, but in presence.

This makes the refrain so striking: There is nothing better than to eat, drink, and enjoy the work of your hands (Ecclesiastes 2:24, 3:13, 5:18). In a world where everything feels fragile, ordinary joy becomes sacred. Every belly laugh with a sistah, every meal shared with a mother or mentor, every friend who stayed when they didn't have to—these are divine gifts. Not rewards for righteousness, but glimmers of God's grace in a groaning world.

Ecclesiastes doesn't shout. It sighs. It grieves. It wonders aloud. This book reads like the quiet reflections of someone who's lived long enough to stop pretending they have all the answers. "Everything is meaningless," the author says in Ecclesiastes 1:2—not because life is void of beauty, but because it's fleeting, unpredictable, beyond our control. Power corrupts. Wealth evaporates. The righteous suffer. And still, we rise each morning and carry on.

Sis, I know you've endured systems that tried to pulverize your spirit. And yet, joy still rises in you. Not the joy that comes from performance, but the joy that sneaks in through a good pot of greens, a fresh hairdo, a cool breeze, or a hug from someone who gets it. That joy is resistance. That joy is faith. That joy is a sacred gift.

The Psalms you read this week echo this truth too. Psalm 103 reminds us that God "remembers we are dust" (Psalm 103:14) and still shows compassion. Psalm 100 calls us to worship with gladness—not after the struggle is over, but right in the middle of it. So when Ecclesiastes closes by saying, "Fear God and keep his commandments" (Ecclesiastes 12:13), it's not a threat. It's an invitation to live well in mystery—to honor God not by mastering life, but by being fully present to it. When nothing else makes sense, obedience becomes an anchor—not to outcomes, but to presence. Faith doesn't erase the fog, but it teaches us how to walk in it with open hands and a soft heart.

SIT WITH IT

1. Ecclesiastes offers wisdom without easy answers. What does it teach you about how to live faithfully even when life feels uncertain or unresolved?

2. Which small joys in your life have you been rushing past or taking for granted? How might you begin honoring them as sacred?

3. Joy can be a form of resistance and healing. How has joy sustained you through difficult seasons, and how can you make space for more of it?

BIBLE TRUTH

Ecclesiastes is part of the Bible's wisdom literature, an ancient genre that reflects on life as it is experienced rather than as it is idealized. The famous refrain "Meaningless! Meaningless!" (Ecclesiastes 1:2) comes from the Hebrew word *hevel*, which means "vapor" or "breath." It appears nearly forty times in Ecclesiastes, reminding us that life is fleeting, fragile, and not always meant to be figured out—only faithfully lived.

WEEK 32

NEGLECTING MY OWN VINEYARD

DAILY READINGS

- Day 1: Song of Songs 1–4
- Day 2: Song of Songs 5–8
- Day 3: Psalms 107–110
- Day 4: Psalms 111–116
- Day 5: Psalms 117–119
- Day 6: Psalms 120–128
- Day 7: Catch up on any readings you've missed.

MOST OF US WERE not taught how to read the Song of Songs. It is often overlooked, skimmed, or under-spiritualized. However, its presence in Scripture is no accident. This is a book about romantic love made flesh, spoken by a sun-kissed woman who is fearless, full of longing, and unafraid to name what she wants.

Song of Songs is unique among biblical texts. It includes no direct mention of God, no miracles, no laws, and no wars—just a sacred celebration of mutual desire and intimacy. Historically attributed to Solomon, it reads more like an anthology of love poems than a religious text. Because of its sheer boldness, this is a book that affirms embodied love as holy. Although its poetic structure flows like a duet, it is the woman's voice that dominates with clarity, confidence, and spiritual depth.

In Song of Songs 1:6, she says, "Do not stare at me because I am dark, because I am darkened by the sun. My mother's sons were angry with me and made me take care of the vineyards; my own vineyard I had to neglect." Her vineyard is her body, her agency, and her very self. And she calls out what so many of us know deep in our bones—being so busy caring for others can make us forget to tend to our own souls.

But do you hear the shift? This is a confession that becomes an opening. The woman in this book isn't passive. She names her desires, claims her beauty, and speaks her boundaries. She offers no apology in her wanting. No shame in her knowing. She is sovereign, sacred, and sensual. Through her voice, we hear the deep echo of Black women across time—carrying communities while being told to deny themselves. She shows us that vulnerability isn't weakness—it's testimony.

She's not whispering. She's singing a hymn we didn't know we needed. A song that reminds us we are allowed to want more than survival; we are allowed to want joy, rest, and care. She dares us to envision a life not just endured but flourishing.

Sis, maybe you've heard this song in your spirit. You've taken every call, shouldered every load, spun every plate—and somewhere along the way, your own vineyard grew wild. You've been celebrated for your strength, but at the expense of your softness. You've learned how to show up, but not how to stay with yourself. So now the Spirit leans close and asks: What would it look like to return to your own care? To rest without guilt? What if your body, your time, and your tenderness were always holy ground?

SIT WITH IT

1. Have you ever resonated with the woman's words in Song of Songs 1:6? What vineyard have you left untended—and why?

2. What beauty, boundary, or dream within you needs to be reclaimed, rewatered, or replanted?

3. Psalm 116:7 says, "Return to your rest, my soul, for the Lord has been good to you." How does this invitation to rest connect with the theme of tending your own vineyard?

SIS, TRY THIS

Choose one small practice this week that tends to your own vineyard. Maybe it's going to bed early without guilt, taking yourself out for lunch, journaling in the sunlight, or saying no without explanation. Let it be simple. Let it be yours. Let it be sacred.

WEEK 33

GOD WITH US, STILL

DAILY READINGS

- Day 1: Isaiah 1–4
- Day 2: Isaiah 5–8
- Day 3: Isaiah 9–12
- Day 4: Isaiah 13–16
- Day 5: Isaiah 17–20
- Day 6: Isaiah 21–24
- Day 7: Catch up on any readings you've missed.

THE BOOK OF ISAIAH isn't light reading—it's a sacred summons. Written across decades of upheaval, Isaiah offers one of the most expansive visions in Scripture. Though traditionally linked to the prophet Isaiah, scholars now understand the book in three parts: chapters 1–39 (First Isaiah) reflect Isaiah's eighth-century-BCE ministry, confronting injustice and idolatry; chapters 40–55 (Second Isaiah) likely speak from exile with messages of comfort; and chapters 56–66 (Third Isaiah) address the hard work of rebuilding a faithful community after return.

This week, we walk through First Isaiah. His opening is raw: God is weary of worship that ignores the suffering of the poor. "Learn to do right; seek justice. Defend the oppressed" (Isaiah 1:17) is the cry. Chapters 1–5 name what's wrong. Chapters 6–12 share Isaiah's own call story and a vision for restoration. Chapters 13–24 warn that judgment isn't reserved for Israel alone—every empire will be held accountable.

In the middle of that chaos, Isaiah utters a promise that still resonates: Immanuel. In Isaiah 7, the prophet speaks to a fearful king. Though Ahaz refuses to ask for a sign, God offers one anyway: "The virgin will conceive and give birth to a son, and will call him Immanuel" (Isaiah 7:14). This was reassurance for Judah—but it has echoed across centuries.

Later, in Isaiah 9:2, we hear: "The people walking in darkness have seen a great light." And the child to come "will be called Wonderful Counselor, Mighty God, Everlasting Father, Prince of Peace" (Isaiah 9:6). These names aren't abstract—they are balm for real wounds. They represent a God who sees deeply and stays close.

Sis, maybe you're walking through your own darkness. Isaiah doesn't dismiss it. He names it—but also names the nearness of God. This isn't the kind of presence that fixes everything overnight. It's the kind that shows up in the thick of it, again and again.

The beauty of Isaiah is that it meets us where we are—in brokenness, fear, or fatigue—and tells the truth. Not everything will be made right immediately. But everything has already been seen. God does not need perfection to draw near. God shows up because we are loved.

You may be too weary to ask for a sign. But God sends one anyway. Not just a miracle, but a steady presence. You're not alone—not now, not ever. God is with you. Still.

SIT WITH IT

1. What does it mean to you that Isaiah's prophecies speaks both judgment and hope in the same breath? How do you hold both?

2. Have you ever felt God's presence in the middle of something chaotic or painful? What did it look or feel like?

3. Reread Isaiah 9:6. Which of the names for the child stands out to you today and why?

VERSE OF THE WEEK

"The virgin will conceive and give birth to a son, and will call him Immanuel."

Isaiah 7:14

WEEK 34
COMFORT IN THE WILDERNESS

DAILY READINGS

- [ ] Day 1: Isaiah 25–27
- [ ] Day 2: Isaiah 28–31
- [ ] Day 3: Isaiah 32–35
- [ ] Day 4: Isaiah 36–39
- [ ] Day 5: Isaiah 40–42
- [ ] Day 6: Isaiah 43–46
- [ ] Day 7: Catch up on any readings you've missed.

YOU'VE MADE IT TO a turning point in the book of Isaiah—and trust me, you'll feel it.

Up to this point, Isaiah has been full of warnings and woe: the unraveling of empires, the corruption of leadership, and the consequences of covenant betrayal. As we saw in last week's reading, this is what scholars call First Isaiah—a prophetic record rooted in Jerusalem before the exile, brimming with judgment and grief.

But something changes in chapter 40. A new voice rises. A different tone emerges. We are no longer in the ruins of what was—we are standing at the edge of what could be. This week we move into Second Isaiah—a section (chapters 40–55) written to a people already in exile. And exile is more than physical relocation. It's disorientation; it's the ache of being where you never planned to be: emotionally, spiritually, or physically. Their temple is gone. Their rhythms disrupted. Their dignity stripped. Everything familiar had been taken—and they are left to rebuild in the shadow of an empire.

Black women know this terrain well, and yet we keep showing up. We keep surviving. But Isaiah reminds us: God didn't just call us to survive.

God spoke into that very heartbreak with a divine declaration: "Comfort, comfort my people, says your God" (Isaiah 40:1).

These are not casual words—they are a prophetic reversal. Where chapters before had declared judgment, now God commands compassion. It is the opening line of a larger vision that restores covenant and renews identity.

It's not a suggestion—it's a summons. God doesn't say endure or wait it out. God says: Comfort them. Tell them they still belong. Tell them I'm still coming.

That comfort isn't passive—it's powerful. It clears space in the wilderness, levels the uneven ground, and declares: "Make straight in the desert a highway for our God" (Isaiah 40:3). In its original context, this wasn't just poetic imagery—it was a metaphor for return. A divine procession was being prepared, not through ideal conditions, but through dry and deserted terrain.

That means exile isn't the end of your story—it might just be the place God reveals the next chapter.

Sis, if you've ever had to praise with tears in your eyes, build while broken, or lead while longing for home, you're not alone. Isaiah is for you. These words were written for exiles, but they're sustained by hope—a hope that doesn't deny the pain, but dares to declare even here, God is near.

So take a deep breath. Let the poetry hold you. Let the promise steady you. This week, may comfort find you in the wilderness.

SIT WITH IT

1. What does "comfort" mean to you in this season—and where are you still waiting to feel it?

____

____

____

2. How have you found a way to speak hope even while carrying hurt?

____

____

____

3. Where in your life does God seem to be preparing a highway in the wilderness?

THIS I PRAY

God of comfort and courage, thank You for meeting me in the places I didn't plan to be. In seasons of exile, when I feel forgotten or far from home, You still speak. Let Your Word steady me this week. Remind me that I am still Yours, even when I feel out of place. Level the ground where I'm weary. Clear a path where I feel stuck. And let Your presence walk beside me through every wilderness. I receive Your comfort—not as a soft escape, but as a sacred strength. In Jesus's name, amen.

WEEK 35

WOUNDED, STILL WORTHY

DAILY READINGS

- Day 1: Isaiah 47–49
- Day 2: Isaiah 50–53
- Day 3: Isaiah 54–57
- Day 4: Isaiah 58–60
- Day 5: Isaiah 61–63
- Day 6: Isaiah 64–66
- Day 7: Catch up on any readings you've missed.

THERE ARE CERTAIN SCRIPTURES that hit a little too close to home. Isaiah 53 is one of them.

This passage describes a suffering servant—a figure "despised and rejected...a man of suffering, and familiar with pain" (Isaiah 53:3). For centuries, Christians have connected this image to Jesus. But before it pointed to Christ, it was a word of comfort and clarity to a people in exile who knew what it meant to be broken.

Isaiah 53:5 says: "He was pierced for our transgressions, he was crushed for our iniquities; the punishment that brought us peace was on him, and by his wounds we are healed." These verses come near the end of Isaiah's fourth and final "servant song." And they don't just describe pain—they confront it. The servant suffers not because of guilt, but on behalf of others. His wounds are not accidental. They become the place where healing begins.

Then we move into Isaiah 61:1—and the voice rises with power: "The Spirit of the Sovereign Lord is on me." This is no longer the servant in sorrow. This is a servant anointed to proclaim good news, bind up wounds, and set captives free. Jesus chose this very passage to launch His public ministry in Luke 4. Why? Because it names both His identity and His mission. And if we're following Him, it becomes our mission too.

By the time you reach Isaiah 56–66, you're in what many call Third Isaiah. The people have returned from exile. But coming home doesn't mean everything is healed. These chapters wrestle with the after—after the crisis, after the return, after the rebuilding. They offer real talk about injustice, inclusion, spiritual complacency, and the call to live with integrity. The work isn't over. The healing continues.

And isn't that real life? Some wounds close slowly. Some seasons of suffering don't come with clean endings. Sometimes we are both the healed and the one in need of healing, the servant and the sent one, the one who aches and the one who announces good news. It's messy—but it's holy. Your healing doesn't have to be finished for you to carry oil for someone else.

Sis, if you've ever wondered whether your pain disqualifies you, hear this: Your wounds don't cancel your worth. You can be both broken and called. God never wastes what you've walked through—and if you're still healing, you're still in good hands. The same Spirit that anointed Jesus is resting on you too.

SIT WITH IT

1. What part of your story still feels wounded, but might be carrying healing for someone else?

2. When have you felt called before you felt ready? How did God meet you in the going?

3. Reflect on Isaiah 56–66. What kind of healing or justice is still unfinished in your life or your community?

BIBLE TRUTH

When Jesus began His public ministry, He opened the scroll of Isaiah and read: "The Spirit of the Lord is on me" (Luke 4:18). By quoting Isaiah 61, Jesus situates His ministry within Israel's prophetic tradition and signals continuity between the Hebrew Scriptures and His public work. Luke uses this moment as a framing scene, establishing healing, liberation, and justice as recurring themes throughout Jesus's ministry.

WEEK 36

SHE PRAYED, SHE SERVED, SHE LED

DAILY READINGS

- Day 1: Acts 1–3
- Day 2: Acts 4–7
- Day 3: Acts 8–10
- Day 4: Acts 11–14
- Day 5: Acts 15–17
- Day 6: Acts 18–21
- Day 7: Catch up on any readings you've missed.

THE BOOK OF ACTS is Luke's continuation of Jesus's ministry, charting the birth of the early Church. It begins with followers gathered in an upper room, waiting and praying. Then, in Acts 2, the Holy Spirit arrives and fills everyone in the room. This isn't a movement reserved for men alone. It is a Holy Spirit–infused uprising powered by prayer, generosity, witness, and radical hospitality—much of it carried by a few women whose names we know, and many more we don't.

Luke makes it plain in Acts 1:14 when he writes, "They all joined together constantly in prayer, along with the women." From the beginning, Mary the mother of Jesus and other women were full participants in the spiritual groundwork of the church.

In Acts we meet Tabitha (Dorcas), "who was always doing good and helping the poor" (Acts 9:36). When she dies, Peter is summoned to Joppa, where grieving widows show him the garments she made for them. Moved by this, Peter prays, and she is restored to life. Her resurrection validates not only her faith, but also her labor—a ministry stitched into the fabric of the community.

In Acts 16, Luke focuses on Lydia, a businesswoman and God-worshipper in Philippi. When Lydia and her household are baptized, she invites Paul and his companions into her home: "If you consider me a believer in the Lord...come and stay at my house" (Acts 16:15). Lydia's home became the first church in Europe, where the mission rested on her spiritual authority, material resources, and bold welcome.

That legacy of discipling women continues well beyond the first church. We see it in our own heritage of Black women like Julia A. J. Foote, born in Schenectady, New York, to formerly enslaved parents. She became the first ordained woman deacon (1894) and the second woman elder (1900) in the AME Zion Church. She spent her days traveling as a preacher during the Holiness revival. Like Lydia, she established space for the gospel to go forward—through tent revivals, in-home devotionals, and the prophetic proclamation that holiness must liberate both soul and society.

Sis, see how the Spirit has always moved through women. From Mary and the praying women, to Tabitha the seamstress, to Lydia the businesswoman, to Julia A. J. Foote the itinerant preacher, women have shaped the church through prayer, service, and sacred hospitality. God uses women to disciple, build, and welcome the people into a faith tradition that changes and transforms lives.

SIT WITH IT

1. Where might God be calling you to use your home, your work, or your voice as sacred space for others?

2. Which woman in this week's devotional—Mary, Tabitha, Lydia, or Julia A. J. Foote—mirrors your season or calling right now?

3. How does reading Acts through the lens of women's leadership shift your understanding of the early Church?

VERSE OF THE WEEK

They all joined together constantly in prayer, along with the women and Mary the mother of Jesus, and with his brothers.

Acts 1:14

WEEK 37
WHEN GOD CALLS

DAILY READINGS

- Day 1: Acts 22–25
- Day 2: Acts 26–28
- Day 3: Jeremiah 1–3
- Day 4: Jeremiah 4–6
- Day 5: Jeremiah 7–11
- Day 6: Jeremiah 12–15
- Day 7: Catch up on any readings you've missed.

WHEN GOD CALLS, EXCUSES won't suffice. From Paul's courtroom testimony to Jeremiah's trembling resistance, Scripture shows us that God doesn't wait for perfection—God moves through obedience.

In Acts 22–28, Paul is arrested, beaten, and falsely accused. Still, he tells his story with boldness, not shame. Once a persecutor of Christians, Paul recounts the moment Jesus interrupted his life through a devout man named Ananias: "Then he said: 'The God of our ancestors has chosen you to know his will... You will be his witness to all people'" (Acts 22:14–15). Paul could have been paralyzed by guilt or fear, but instead, he accepts grace and steps into God's assignment—even under threat, even in chains.

Jeremiah's calling begins in protest. In Jeremiah 1:5, God says: "Before I formed you in the womb I knew you, before you were born I set you apart." Still, Jeremiah replies, "I do not know how to speak; I am too young" (Jeremiah 1:6). But God insists: "Do not say, 'I am too young'... I am with you and will rescue you" (Jeremiah 1:7–8). And then comes the divine touch: "I have put my words in your mouth" (Jeremiah 1:9). Jeremiah's "yes" launched decades of discipleship under pressure. He wept over injustice, stood against corrupt kings, and called his community to repentance with love and clarity. Chapters 1–15 reveal a prophet who feels deeply, speaks truth fiercely, and never walks alone. His fears aren't erased, but God uses them to strengthen his ministry.

That same clarity anchored Rev. Dr. Prathia Hall—a preacher, scholar, and civil rights warrior. As a young activist with the Student Nonviolent Coordinating Committee, she faced threats and firebombs while organizing voter drives in the rural South. But her voice was unmistakable. It was Hall's prayer, spoken in a 1962 prayer meeting in Terrell County, Georgia, that first used the phrase "I have a dream." Before it was Martin's dream, it was Prathia's prayer—a prophetic utterance that deeply impacted Dr. King. Later, Hall reflected: "I stood in the authenticity of my being: Black, preacher, Baptist, woman. For the same God who made me a preacher made me a woman, and I am convinced that God was not confused on either account."

Sis, excuses don't exempt you—they expose where faith must rise. God isn't confused about who you are. Your voice belongs here. Your witness matters. Whether you feel young like Jeremiah, unworthy like Paul, or out of place like Hall once did—your "yes" is sacred. Whatever the call, your obedience creates space for others to believe, be free, and be changed. No more delays. Say yes.

SIT WITH IT

1. What excuse—spoken or unspoken—has been holding you back from saying yes to your call?

2. Where in your life has fear been louder than faith? How might Jeremiah's story help you move anyway?

3. How does Rev. Dr. Hall's "authenticity of being" challenge or affirm the way you show up in ministry, leadership, or service?

THIS I PRAY

God, I hear You calling me—even when I feel unready. Quiet my fears. Strengthen my "yes." Like Jeremiah, let me speak with courage. Like Paul, let me stand in truth. Like Rev. Dr. Hall, let me rise in the fullness of who I am. Use me, Lord. I'm willing. In Jesus's name I pray, amen.

WEEK 38

CALLED IN A CRISIS

DAILY READINGS

- Day 1: Jeremiah 16–19
- Day 2: Jeremiah 20–22
- Day 3: Jeremiah 23–26
- Day 4: Jeremiah 27–30
- Day 5: Jeremiah 31–34
- Day 6: Jeremiah 35–37
- Day 7: Catch up on any readings you've missed.

JEREMIAH WAS NEVER THE people's favorite prophet. Although others offered visions of quick relief, he came with a yoke around his neck—literally—prophesying long-term captivity. A yoke is a heavy wooden crosspiece used to link two oxen together, often symbolizing burden, control, or submission. In Jeremiah 27, God instructs Jeremiah to wear one as a prophetic act: The people must submit to Babylon, or they'll be crushed for resisting it.

Then in chapter 28, Hananiah rises. This polished and persuasive priest grabs the wooden yoke off Jeremiah and breaks it. He declares that in two years, God will bring the people home.

It sounds good. But it's not true.

Jeremiah walks away silently at first. But God sends him back with a sharper word: "You have broken a wooden yoke, but in its place you will get a yoke of iron" (Jeremiah 28:13). The truth hasn't changed—it's just heavier.

By the time we reach the infamous chapter 29, Jeremiah delivers a letter to those already in exile. And his message is not what they expected. He tells them to build homes. Plant gardens. Raise children. Seek the peace of Babylon. In short: Settle in. Not as captives of despair, but as witnesses with a blueprint.

Then comes the line we love to quote: "'For I know the plans I have for you,' declares the Lord, "plans to prosper you and not to harm you, plans to give you hope and a future" (Jeremiah 29:11). But let's sit with it fully. These words were not spoken to people on the edge of breakthrough, but to those deep in the middle of loss. God's idea of prosperity wasn't quick relief—it was resilient living. Hope wasn't framed as escape—it was endurance with purpose. "A future" didn't mean immediate change—it meant divine investment that would unfold over time. That promise wasn't empty comfort—it was a call to keep building anyway.

We've seen this lived out before. In the 1870s, thousands of formerly enslaved people left the South and headed west, seeking peace and land. They became known as "Exodusters." It wasn't easy.

The terrain was rough. Winters were brutal. And yet, they persevered. They dug wells, planted crops, educated children, and worshipped in brush arbors. Some towns, like Nicodemus, Kansas, survived. Others faded. But the testimony stands: They trusted that God still had plans—even in exile.

Maybe you're in your own Babylon, planted in unfamiliar soil. But hear me: Exile doesn't cancel your calling. It clarifies it. You are still seen. You are still sent. And yes—God still has plans for you.

SIT WITH IT

1. Where have you been tempted to cling to a version of faith that promised quick escape instead of honest endurance?

2. What does it look like to build, plant, or stay present in a place that doesn't match what you prayed for?

3. Jeremiah 29:11 is often quoted, but rarely wrestled with. What does it mean for you to trust God's plan when the future feels delayed, distant, or unfamiliar?

SIS, TRY THIS

This week, take a moment to write Jeremiah 29:11 as if God were saying it directly to you—not as a shortcut to blessing, but as a promise to be present right where you are. Begin with, "I know the plans I have for you" and then let the Spirit lead. Let it be raw, rooted, and real.

WEEK 39

COURAGE IN THE PALACE

DAILY READINGS

- [ ] Day 1: Jeremiah 38–41
- [ ] Day 2: Jeremiah 42–45
- [ ] Day 3: Jeremiah 46–49
- [ ] Day 4: Jeremiah 50–52
- [ ] Day 5: Lamentations 1–2
- [ ] Day 6: Lamentations 3–5
- [ ] Day 7: Catch up on any readings you've missed.

THERE IS SOMETHING PECULIAR in chapter 38 of Jeremiah. The prophet of God has been faithful, yet instead of honor he finds himself sinking into mud at the bottom of a pit for speaking truth to power. Everyone knows the act is unjust, but no one dares intervene—except Ebed-Melek. He goes to the king and says, "These men have acted wickedly in all they have done to Jeremiah the prophet. They have thrown him into a cistern, where he will starve to death when there is no longer any bread in the city" (Jeremiah 38:8).

Let's understand the risk here. Ebed-Melek is African, a Cushite from the region of modern-day Sudan or Ethiopia. He is a servant in the palace, not a ruler. To approach the king and declare that the officials have acted wickedly is dangerous. His position, his livelihood, even his life could be taken for speaking against the establishment. Yet he goes boldly in verse 9 to the king and says, in essence, "This is wrong! Jeremiah will die if you do nothing."

This isn't just courage—it's also compassion. When the king allows Jeremiah's rescue, Ebed-Melek lowers ropes into the pit. But before pulling Jeremiah up, he also lowers rags. "Put these old rags and worn-out clothes under your arms to pad the ropes" (Jeremiah 38:12) he tells the prophet. Ebed-Melek could simply snatch Jeremiah out, but he takes care not to cause unnecessary harm. Without those protective wraps, the prophet's skin would have been cut, the ropes leaving bruises.

This is powerful because sometimes deliverance comes rough, fast, and messy. We survive, but we're left bruised and bleeding. Ebed-Melek shows us another way. He teaches us that courage without compassion can still wound. But when you trust God enough to act with both boldness and tenderness, you embody the kind of deliverance that not only saves life but also preserves dignity.

Later, Jeremiah delivers a personal word from God to Ebed-Melek: "I will rescue you...because you trust in me" (Jeremiah 39:17–18). The one who rescued Jeremiah is himself rescued.

The one who refused to let the prophet's body be battered is himself spared.

Sis, maybe you're the one in a pit right now: sinking, unseen, unjustly treated. Hear this: God will not only lift you up but will also cover you, shielding you from further harm. Or maybe you're the one called to be like Ebed-Melek, stepping into risky places to speak truth and help someone else rise. Either way, know this: Deliverance is coming—and God's protection comes with it.

SIT WITH IT

1. Where might God be asking you to speak up with both courage and compassion, even if it feels risky?

2. Have you ever experienced a "rough deliverance" that left you bruised? What would it mean to trust that God can deliver with tenderness too?

3. Which role resonates with you right now—Jeremiah in the pit, or Ebed-Melek at the rope? Why?

BIBLE TRUTH

Ebed-Melek appears in the final chapters of the book of Jeremiah, during the fall of Jerusalem. His actions are recorded in Jeremiah 38 and affirmed again in Jeremiah 39, where God promises to protect him because of his trust. His name means "servant of the king," yet Ebed-Melek chose to serve the King of kings by acting with justice and compassion. Identified as a Cushite of North African origin, his presence in Scripture reminds us that Black people have always been part of God's redemptive story.

WEEK 40
SANCTUARY IN STRANGE PLACES

DAILY READINGS

- Day 1: Ezekiel 1–3
- Day 2: Ezekiel 4–7
- Day 3: Ezekiel 8–11
- Day 4: Ezekiel 12–15
- Day 5: Ezekiel 16–18
- Day 6: Ezekiel 19–21
- Day 7: Catch up on any readings you've missed.

SIS, I BET YOU know something about exile. Not necessarily leaving your land, but being pushed to the margins—at work, at church, in family systems that didn't make room for you. You've felt what it is to live far from center, to wonder if the cycles of the past are unbreakable. But listen: God is a sanctuary wherever you are. Not just in stained glass or pulpits. Sanctuary can be your kitchen table, your morning commute, the quiet corner of your apartment, or the whispered prayer before you walk into a meeting. God travels with you.

Ezekiel's ministry begins in captivity. Jerusalem has fallen to Babylon, and leaders, artisans, and families are marched out of their homes into a foreign land. They are broken, scattered, and cut off from the temple—the place they thought God lived. Imagine the shock: the house of God in ruins, their routines shattered, their identity undone. Exile is not only about geography—it's about losing the center, the sense of belonging, the feeling of security.

This week's readings walk us through Ezekiel's wild visions and prophetic acts. In chapter 1, he sees wheels within wheels; fire that cannot be contained; glory that's on the move. In chapters 4–7, he enacts judgment for the people's sin. Then in chapters 8–11, he sees corruption in the temple, the very place meant for holiness. But in the midst of it all God speaks a word of hope: "Although I sent them far away among the nations…for a little while I have been a sanctuary for them in the countries where they have gone" (Ezekiel 11:16). God is saying: *I am not confined to the temple. I am with you—even in exile.*

Later in chapter 18, another word cuts through despair. The people repeat a proverb: "The parents eat sour grapes, and the children's teeth are set on edge" (Ezekiel 18:2). In other words: *We're doomed by what came before us.* But God interrupts: "Repent and live!" (Ezekiel 18:32). Each life is still open. History matters, but it does not dictate the end. Even in exile, renewal is possible.

And like those exiles, you are not condemned by what came before. You are not the proverb of "sour grapes." Generational curses don't define you. Renewal is stronger than history. You can turn. You can pivot. You can live.

Sis, exile may feel like forever—but it is not godless. Sanctuary travels with you. Even here, there is hope and accountability; there is still the invitation to repent, turn, live.

SIT WITH IT

1. Where do you feel like you're living in exile—not geographically, but emotionally, spiritually, or relationally?

2. What "sour grapes" have you been told define your life? How might God be inviting you to release that story?

3. Where have you discovered an unexpected sanctuary—a place or moment where God showed up outside traditional walls?

THIS I PRAY

God of every place, thank You for being a sanctuary even in exile. When life feels scattered, when the center is gone, remind me that You are near. Break every lie that says the past binds my future. Teach me to repent, to turn, to live. And wherever I find myself—on the margins, in the wilderness, or on the way home—let me rest in Your presence. In Jesus's name, amen.

WEEK 41

WHEN DRY BONES LIVE AGAIN

DAILY READINGS

- Day 1: Ezekiel 22–24
- Day 2: Ezekiel 25–28
- Day 3: Ezekiel 29–32
- Day 4: Ezekiel 33–36
- Day 5: Ezekiel 37–39
- Day 6: Ezekiel 40–42
- Day 7: Catch up on any readings you've missed.

BY THE TIME WE get to Ezekiel 37, hope is worn out and Jerusalem is gone. The people have been dragged off to Babylon. Despair is thick and heavy in the air. Then God takes the prophet into a valley full of bones. They are dry and brittle—forgotten even. "Son of man, can these bones live?" God asks. Ezekiel doesn't sugarcoat it. "Sovereign Lord, you alone know" (Ezekiel 37:3).

Then comes the strangest command from God: "Prophesy to these bones and say to them, 'Dry bones, hear the word of the Lord!'"(Ezekiel 37:4). So he speaks, and the bones begin to rattle. Bone to bone. Then muscle. Skin. But still no breath. Then God commands again: "Prophesy to the breath" (Ezekiel 37:9) and suddenly breath rushes in. They rise to their feet. They are a vast army (Ezekiel 37:10).

This isn't a figment of the prophet's imagination. God makes it plain: "These bones are the people of Israel. They say, 'Our bones are dried up and our hope is gone; we are cut off...' 'I will put my Spirit in you and you will live'" (Ezekiel 37:11, 14).

If you've lived long enough, you've probably known a valley or two. A season when dreams dry out. When faith feels brittle. When grief, betrayal, or just the grind of keeping everyone else standing leaves you bone tired. The truth is, God still speaks in valleys. God still breathes where life looks impossible. Restoration isn't tidy. It shakes. It rumbles. It disrupts. But when God breathes, what we thought was gone can stand again.

Fannie Lou Hamer—a sharecropper's daughter from the Mississippi Delta who rose to become a leading voice in the Civil Rights Movement—knew about dry bones. In 1963, she was beaten nearly to death in a Mississippi jail for trying to register to vote. Her face carried the scars. Her voice was dismissed. But she would not quit. With holy defiance she said, "I'm sick and tired of being sick and tired." From that valley, her witness stirred the nation awake. Her life preached Ezekiel's vision—the Spirit rising through what the world tried to bury.

Sis, the valley is not the finale. Dry bones can live again. It might be messy. It might be loud. But the Spirit is still moving. Believe God can revive what feels beyond repair. Believe that breath will return. And when it does, you will rise—not on your own, but as living proof that hope never died.

SIT WITH IT

1. Where have you felt like you were standing in a valley of dry bones—tired, brittle, or cut off?

 ____

 ____

2. How do you imagine God's breath moving through the places in your life that feel hopeless?

 ____

 ____

3. What does Fannie Lou Hamer's story stir in you about resilience and faith?

 ____

 ____

VERSE OF THE WEEK

""I will put my Spirit in you and you will live."

Ezekiel 37:14

WEEK 42

FAITH THAT WON'T BOW

DAILY READINGS

- Day 1: Ezekiel 43–45
- Day 2: Ezekiel 46–48
- Day 3: Daniel 1–4
- Day 4: Daniel 5–8
- Day 5: Daniel 9–12
- Day 6: Psalms 129–135
- Day 7: Catch up on any readings you've missed.

THE BOOK OF DANIEL is a story of faith under intense government pressure. Daniel and his friends are strangers in a foreign land, taken from Judah into Babylon. They are pressured to conform to the culture and the commands of those in power. Some chapters read like dramatic stories: a fiery furnace, a lion's den, handwriting on the wall. Others contain visions pointing toward God's ultimate reign. What ties the book together is this: God's power is always greater, and faithful living is always possible.

In Daniel 3, the pressure is on and the message is clear: Bow or burn. But three young men—Shadrach, Meshach, and Abednego—refuse. Their response is, "The God we serve is able to deliver us... But even if he does not, we want you to know, Your Majesty, that we will not serve your gods" (Daniel 3:17–18). They are thrown into the furnace, but a fourth figure appears beside them. They walk out unsinged. God is with them in the fire.

In Daniel 6, King Darius signs a decree forbidding prayer to anyone except him. This time the command is not to bow but to stop. Daniel refuses. "Three times a day he got down on his knees and prayed, giving thanks to his God, just as he had done before" (Daniel 6:10). For this act of rebellion, Daniel is thrown into the lions' den, but the lions' mouths are shut. Daniel emerges alive. God is with him in the den.

One story says, "Bow to what is false." The other, "Stop what is true." Faith that holds on to God won't do either, and in both cases, God's presence proved stronger than the pressure.

Black women know this kind of faith. We've been told to bow: bow to silence, bow to respectability, bow to roles that diminish us. We've also been told to stop—stop praying, stop leading, stop speaking truth to power. Yet, like Daniel and his friends, we don't have to give in.

Think of Stacey Abrams, a leading figure in today's political landscape and a tireless advocate for voting rights. She faced fierce opposition but refused to bow to pressure or stop her work. When doors closed, she built new ones, creating organizations that registered hundreds of thousands of voters across Georgia and beyond. Her persistence shifted history. She shows us God is still present when the fire gets hot and when the lions roar.

Sis, your faith doesn't have to look polished to be powerful. Sometimes it looks like saying no when everyone else bows. Sometimes it looks like praying when everyone else goes quiet. Either way, you are not alone. The same God who stood in the furnace and shut the lions' mouths is standing with you still.

SIT WITH IT

1. Where do you feel pressured to "bow"—to conform, stay silent, or play small?

____

____

____

2. Where are you being tempted to "stop"—to stop praying, stop leading, stop showing up in your fullness?

____

____

____

3. What would it look like to trust God's presence with you in the fire or in the den? How might remembering that God is standing beside you change the way you respond to pressure?

____

____

____

SIS, TRY THIS

1. Take some time to reflect on one place in your life where you feel pressure to bow or temptation to stop. Write it down in your journal.
2. Then, underneath it, write: "I will not bow. I will not stop."
3. Pray over those words this week, asking God for courage to hold steady, especially in moments when standing firm feels hardest.

WEEK 43

GOD KNOWS, GOD WORKS

DAILY READINGS

- Day 1: Psalms 136–142
- Day 2: Psalms 143–150
- Day 3: Romans 1–4
- Day 4: Romans 5–8
- Day 5: Romans 9–12
- Day 6: Romans 13–16
- Day 7: Catch up on any readings you've missed.

LIFE DOESN'T ALWAYS FEEL harmonious. Some days feel scattered, unpredictable, or out of our control. But in the middle of that uncertainty, there's a steady truth: God is already present, already weaving, already writing a story bigger than what we can see.

In Psalm 139, we hear David's confession that his life is not random. God has already searched him, known him, and written his story. He says, "All the days ordained for me were written in your book before one of them came to be" (Psalm 139:16). David trusts his future not because he can see it, but because God can. Even in the dark, David reminds us that God is still present. Even when David runs, God is still near.

Paul echoes this same confidence in Romans 8. Speaking to believers who knew struggle, he reminds them: "We know that in all things God works for the good of those who love him" (Romans 8:28). That doesn't mean everything feels good in the moment, but it does mean nothing is wasted. God is weaving even the hardest days into something that will make sense in time. Waiting, then, is not wasted time—it is discipleship in motion, trusting that God is still at work even when we cannot see the outcome.

Put together, these passages are a promise you can hang your hat on: God knows, and God works. Psalm 139 says your future is already assured. Romans 8 is a reminder to give God time to work it together for your good and for God's glory.

And that's the hard part, isn't it? Trusting God in the waiting—when doors close, answers feel delayed, and the story doesn't make sense yet. But patience in the waiting is still faith—it's believing that the Author who wrote your story has not stopped editing it for good.

Black women know this kind of waiting. We carry families, lead movements, and hold communities together while our own futures feel uncertain. We are asked to trust when resources are thin, to stand steady when outcomes are slow to arrive, to believe when others doubt. Psalm 139 reminds us that every day of our lives is already known by God. Romans 8 reminds us that even that which looks scattered is still in God's hands.

Sis, you don't have to control every detail or rush the process. God has already seen your future, and God is still working the pieces together. Trust that what feels unfinished today is not the end. In time, you will see how even this season was stitched into something good.

SIT WITH IT

1. David testifies in Psalm 139 that God is with him in every place—light or dark, near or far. How do you identify with that testimony in your own life? Where have you seen God's presence in both the good and the hard seasons?

2. Romans 12:1 calls us to present our bodies as a "living sacrifice," our spiritual act of worship. How might offering your waiting season to God as worship help you practice patience?

3. Think of a time when something in your past looked scattered but later revealed God's hand at work. How does remembering that moment strengthen your faith today?

VERSE OF THE WEEK

We know that in all things God works for the good of those who love him.

Romans 8:28

WEEK 44

RETURN, RESTORE, REDEFINE

- ☐ Daily Readings
- ☐ Day 1: Hosea 1–5
- ☐ Day 2: Hosea 6–10
- ☐ Day 3: Hosea 11–14
- ☐ Day 4: Joel 1–3
- ☐ Day 5: Amos 1–5
- ☐ Day 6: Amos 6–9
- ☐ Day 7: Catch up on any readings you've missed.

WE'VE ALL HAD MOMENTS where we wished we could start again. A season we'd love to redo, years we thought were wasted, or a version of ourselves we hoped would be different. That longing for renewal is real—and it's not foreign to God. Scripture reminds us that the final word is never failure. With God, there is always a way back, a way forward, a way made new.

Hosea's last chapter brings the hope of renewal to life. After all the warnings, after all the heartbreak, the final word is not rejection but invitation. "Return, Israel, to the Lord your God. Your sins have been your downfall! Take words with you and return to the Lord" (Hosea 14:1–2). Return is the beginning. Not shame or despair—just turning back toward the One who can heal. And God promises: "I will heal their waywardness and love them freely" (Hosea 14:4). That is the heart of God. Not ruin, but restoration.

Joel carries that same theme in chapter 2. After devastation so complete it seems like life itself is gone, God speaks through Joel: "I will repay you for the years the locusts have eaten" (Joel 2:25). God can bring back seasons that look finished, dreams that seem too far gone. Return leads to restoration.

But Joel doesn't stop there. Restoration comes with redefinition. God says: "I will pour out my Spirit on all people. Your sons and daughters will prophesy, your old men will dream dreams, your young men will see visions. Even on my servants, both men and women, I will pour out my Spirit in those days" (Joel 2:28–29). This is radical. Prophecy had been seen as the domain of men with power. But here, daughters are named. Servants are named. Everyone is included.

Return. Restore. Redefine. That is the rhythm of God's promise.

Black women know all three. We know what it is to return after heartbreak or mistakes and to find that God's arms are still open. We know what it means to plead for restoration when struggle seems to have eaten up years of our lives—yet we believe those years weren't lost. And we know redefinition, because the world has told us too often that our voices don't matter, our leadership isn't wanted. But Joel says otherwise. Daughters prophesy. Servants dream. Women carry God's Spirit just as fully as anyone else.

Sis, maybe this is your time to return. Maybe you are waiting for restoration. Or maybe you need to be reminded that God has already redefined who you are and what you carry. Wherever you stand, hear this: God's love is still calling. God's Spirit is still moving. And God's promise still includes you.

SIT WITH IT

1. Hosea 14 reminds us that God's invitation is to return, not with shame but with hope. Where in your life do you sense God calling you back for healing?

2. Joel 2 promises that God will restore what locusts have eaten. What years, seasons, or dreams do you long for God to redeem?

3. God pours out the Spirit on all people—sons and daughters, young and old, servants and free. How does this redefinition of who is included affirm your own voice and calling today?

BIBLE TRUTH

Joel's prophecy was originally spoken to a community recovering from devastation. In Acts 2, Peter quotes Joel 2:28–29 to interpret the outpouring of the Holy Spirit at Pentecost, naming it as God's promise unfolding in real time. What Joel proclaimed centuries earlier comes alive as the Holy Spirit is poured out on women and men, young and old alike—confirming that God's Spirit is not reserved for a few but given to all.

WEEK 45

THE CRY OF "HOW LONG?"

DAILY READINGS

- ☐ Day 1: Obadiah 1
- ☐ Day 2: Jonah 1–4
- ☐ Day 3: Micah 1–4
- ☐ Day 4: Micah 5–7
- ☐ Day 5: Nahum 1–3
- ☐ Day 6: Habakkuk 1–3
- ☐ Day 7: Catch up on any readings you've missed.

MICAH WAS A PROPHET who spoke hard truths to Israel and to us. He made it plain that God's expectations are not confusing or hidden. Micah leaves us with no doubt about God's expectations. When the people wonder what God wants—sacrifices, rituals, offerings—Micah cuts through the noise: "He has shown you, O mortal, what is good. And what does the Lord require of you? To act justly and to love mercy and to walk humbly with your God" (Micah 6:8). That isn't optional or extra. Justice, mercy, and humility are the life God calls us to live.

But Habakkuk reminds us that justice is never easy. He begins with lament: "How long, Lord, must I call for help, but you do not listen?" (Habakkuk 1:2). He names the violence and destruction around him. God's reply is not a quick fix but a call to trust: "The righteous person will live by faithfulness" (Habakkuk 2:4). Justice is the requirement, but faith is the posture in the waiting.

This tension is familiar to Black women. We carry Micah's call to act justly and love mercy in our homes, workplaces, and communities. And we know Habakkuk's cry, because we, too, have asked, "How long?" How long will our lives be undervalued? How long will systems fail to serve and protect us?

When we say the names Breonna Taylor and Sandra Bland, we join Habakkuk's lament. Both were Black women whose lives were cut short in ways that demand justice. Their names remind us that "how long?" is not rhetorical—it is urgent, embodied, right now. And yet in their memory we also hear Micah's call: Keep pressing for justice, keep walking humbly, keep showing mercy, because this is what God requires.

I grew up in the United Church of Christ (UCC), a denomination that has long carried justice as one of its cornerstones. I think of Rev. Traci D. Blackmon, a UCC minister from St. Louis who stood boldly in Ferguson after the tragic shooting of Michael Brown Jr. She reminded the nation of Micah's mandate—that the gospel cannot be separated from justice. To be Spirit-filled in worship but silent in the streets is to miss God's call. Justice work is God's work.

Sis, living as a Black woman of faith means carrying both Micah and Habakkuk. It means acting justly, even when change comes slow; keeping faith, even when the waiting feels unbearable. It means we cry out, "How long?" and still believe God hears.

We don't have to choose between the work and the waiting, or between the demand for justice and the discipline of faith. Both belong to us. Both are holy. Both are how we walk with God.

SIT WITH IT

1. Micah 6:8 makes God's requirement clear: justice, mercy, humility. Which one feels most natural for you to practice, and which one feels hardest right now?

2. Habakkuk's cry, "How long, Lord?" echoes in our own lives. Where do you feel yourself asking this same question today?

3. How does carrying Micah's call to do justice and Habakkuk's call to live by faith together shape your walk with God?

VERSE OF THE WEEK

He has shown you, O mortal, what is good. And what does the Lord require of you? To act justly and to love mercy and to walk humbly with your God.

Micah 6:8

WEEK 46

LET LOVE REACH YOU

DAILY READINGS

- Day 1: 1 Corinthians 1–4
- Day 2: 1 Corinthians 5–8
- Day 3: 1 Corinthians 9–12
- Day 4: 1 Corinthians 13–16
- Day 5: 2 Corinthians 1–6
- Day 6: 2 Corinthians 7–13
- Day 7: Catch up on any readings you've missed.

THE CHURCH IN CORINTH had no shortage of talent. They prized knowledge, eloquence, and spiritual gifts. But Paul reminds them, while addressing their divisions and questions about food sacrificed to idols: "Knowledge puffs up while love builds up" (1 Corinthians 8:1). What matters is not how much you know or how gifted you appear, but whether love is shaping—or being shaped by—your life.

That theme runs through the entire letter, and after teaching on the one body and many gifts, it reaches its high point in chapter 13. After naming gifts like tongues, prophecy, and knowledge, Paul makes it plain: Without love, it all falls flat. "If I speak in the tongues of men or of angels, but do not have love, I am only a resounding gong or a clanging cymbal" (1 Corinthians 13:1). Without love, all the things we celebrate—gifts, skills, leadership—become empty noise.

We often read Paul's words as a checklist of what love *does*: Love is patient, love is kind, love endures. But what if we also read them as a description of the love we are meant to *receive*? Black women in particular are often taught that love must be earned through how much we do, how much we sacrifice, or how much we hold everything together. But Paul reminds us we are worthy of a love that protects, perseveres, and never fails. We are not only called to give this kind of love—we are worthy and deserving of it. Paul's words are not just a mandate for what you owe others, but a mirror of what God intends you to receive.

I learned this in a profound way during my sixteen-week sabbatical in 2022. I was navigating divorce, traveling the world, carrying questions about what I truly deserved. When I went to Bali with my girlfriends, I experienced intimacy and care in a way I hadn't known before. I realized I wasn't just giving love—I was receiving it. These women didn't just say they loved me; they showed it. They bore the fruit of love in their actions. In other seasons, I had settled for words without evidence, promises without proof, and violations without repentance. But on that trip, I knew what it meant to experience love and let it wash over me.

Sis, discipleship isn't only about pouring love out. It's also about making sure you allow yourself to receive the kind of love Paul describes—the kind God designed you for. Titles will fade. Achievements will pass. "Do everything in love" (1 Corinthians 16:14), Paul concludes. That includes letting love reach you.

SIT WITH IT

1. When you read Paul's words in 1 Corinthians 13, do you usually think of them as what you are meant to do or what you are meant to receive in your life? How does that shift shape the way you see God's love at work in you?

2. Paul warns in 1 Corinthians 8:1 that "knowledge puffs up while love builds up," drawing a clear contrast between the two. Where do you see this contrast today—in the church, in community, or even in yourself? What would it mean to choose love over pride or performance?

3. Can you identify spaces, friendships, or communities where you have truly received love that bears fruit? What does that kind of love teach you about God's heart?

THIS I PRAY

God of love, teach me to see myself as worthy of the love You describe. Free me from believing I have to earn what You have already given. Surround me with people who don't just speak love but show it, and help me to recognize and receive those gifts without fear or hesitation. In Jesus's name, amen.

WEEK 47

TRUST GOD FOR THE REST

DAILY READINGS

- ☐ Day 1: Zephaniah 1–3
- ☐ Day 2: Haggai 1–2
- ☐ Day 3: Zechariah 1–5
- ☐ Day 4: Zechariah 6–10
- ☐ Day 5: Zechariah 11–14
- ☐ Day 6: Malachi 1–4
- ☐ Day 7: Catch up on any readings you've missed.

WE ALL KNOW THOSE seasons when nothing seems to work. Bills stack up. Relationships feel fragile. Plans unravel. In those moments, we wonder if we will ever get back on track. That is when God's Word breaks in with a call to rebuild. That is the message we hear in the book of Haggai.

By the time we reach the minor prophet Haggai, the people have returned from exile in Babylon and are rebuilding life in Jerusalem after years of displacement, loss, and interrupted worship. But while their own houses are carefully tended, God's house lies in ruins. Through the prophet, God asks a piercing question: "Is it a time for you yourselves to be living in your paneled houses, while this house remains a ruin?" (Haggai 1:4). The call is clear: Reorder your priorities, and place God first. And with that call comes a promise: "The glory of this present house will be greater than the glory of the former house" (Haggai 2:9).

Malachi, the final prophet before the New Testament, speaks to a weary community that has grown casual in its worship. They bring blemished sacrifices and hold back their best. God responds not by abandoning them but by purifying them, promising to send "my messenger" (Malachi 3:1) who…"will sit as a refiner and purifier of silver" (Malachi 3:3). And God adds hope for the faithful: "But for you who revere my name, the sun of righteousness will rise with healing in its rays. And you will go out and frolic like well-fed calves." (Malachi 4:2).

Together, Haggai and Malachi remind us that discipleship is not about offering God what is left over. It is about giving God our best—our best attention, our best devotion, our best selves—and trusting God to do the rest.

Black women know this rhythm well. Many of us remember our grandmothers rising early before anyone else in the house stirred, Bible open, whispering prayers in the kitchen over coffee. In fact, my grandmother had a chair that we all knew was where she prayed and sought the Lord. Before the weight of the day fell on their shoulders, many of the women we've come from offered God their first and best. It was their way of saying, "I trust You to handle what I cannot."

Sis, the fact that you've made it all the way to week 47 is a sign that this same commitment now lives in you. You have chosen again and again to give God your time, your energy, your attention. That is no small thing. And the promise of these prophets still holds: When you give God your best, God will refine, restore, and make the future greater than the past.

Trust God for the rest.

SIT WITH IT

1. In Haggai, God asks the people why their houses are thriving while God's house is in ruins. Where might your priorities need realignment to put God first?

____

____

____

2. Malachi speaks of someone that God will send who will be like a refiner of pure silver. Where in your life do you sense God refining you—polishing, purifying, shaping you for greater wholeness?

____

____

____

3. Think about your own family history. Do you have memories of a grandmother, mother, or mentor who modeled giving God their best? What do those memories stir in you now?

SIS, TRY THIS

If you don't usually rise early, let this be the week you try it. Set aside one morning to wake up before the house stirs and give God the first part of your day. And if you already rise early, I encourage you to set aside at least ten minutes in pure silence, simply listening for God. What if you offered God your ears first, before you ask for anything, before you say a word?

WEEK 48

RISE AND REBUILD

DAILY READINGS

- Day 1: Ezra 1–5
- Day 2: Ezra 6–10
- Day 3: Nehemiah 1–3
- Day 4: Nehemiah 4–7
- Day 5: Nehemiah 8–10
- Day 6: Nehemiah 11–13
- Day 7: Catch up on any readings you've missed.

THE BOOK OF NEHEMIAH is about rebuilding in the aftermath of loss. God's people have come home from exile, but the walls of Jerusalem are still broken and the gates lie in ashes. The city is exposed and vulnerable, a painful reminder of everything they have lost. Into this moment, God raises up Nehemiah—an ordinary man who works as cupbearer to the king—who answers the call to rebuild what was ruined.

When Nehemiah hears how broken Jerusalem is, he breaks down in tears. He fasts, prays, and mourns before God (Nehemiah 1:3–4). Out of that place of lament, courage begins to rise. Later, when opponents try to intimidate the builders, Nehemiah tells the people: "Don't be afraid of them. Remember the Lord, who is great and awesome, and fight for your families, your sons and your daughters, your wives and your homes" (Nehemiah 4:14).

Rebuilding is never simple. It is messy, slow, and risky. Yet the wall goes up because the people hold grief in one hand and bricks in the other. That, my Sis, is resilience.

We know something about that kind of rubble. The loss of someone we love. The end of a marriage. Losing a job. Or watching our most basic expectations of life crumble into pieces. What once felt steady now lies scattered, and like Nehemiah, we begin with tears. With lament. With the honest cry: *This is not how it was supposed to be.*

But lament is not the ending—for Israel or for you. God calls us to rebuild, not by erasing the past but by daring to believe that life can grow again from ruins. After my divorce, rebuilding meant grieving the future I thought I'd have, asking hard questions I never imagined, and then slowly piecing together a new vision of what was possible. That work came brick by brick, prayer by prayer, fast by fast, small act of courage by small act of courage—until I could see that God was building something strong beneath my feet.

Sis, maybe you're in that season now. Maybe you're staring at something that feels unfixable. Hear me: Your resilience is holy.

To grieve and to build is an act of discipleship. The God who strengthened Nehemiah is strengthening you.

And remember: The wall wasn't rebuilt in a day, and it wasn't rebuilt alone. Scripture says "the people worked with all their heart" (Nehemiah 4:6). God will send help—friends, family, sacred community—to lift bricks beside you.

What was broken can rise again. And so can you.

SIT WITH IT

1. Nehemiah wept before he built. Where in your life do you need to give yourself permission to lament before rushing into action?

2. Think of a time when something in your life had to be rebuilt after loss, disappointment, or change. What helped you take those first "bricks" in hand?

3. Scripture says "the people worked with all their heart" (Nehemiah 4:6). Who are the people in your sacred community who can help you rebuild? How might you lean on them?

BIBLE TRUTH

When Nehemiah first heard the news about Jerusalem's broken walls, he fasted and prayed (Nehemiah 1:4). Fasting in Scripture is never just about food—it is about focus. It creates space to lament, to listen for God, and to align our hearts with God's purposes. That practice is still relevant today. Whether by abstaining from food, social media, or other distractions, fasting reminds us that rebuilding begins not with our strength but with God's.

WEEK 49

THE PRICE OF FREEDOM

DAILY READINGS

- Day 1: Galatians 1–6
- Day 2: Ephesians 1–6
- Day 3: Philippians 1–4
- Day 4: Colossians 1–4
- Day 5: 1 Thessalonians 1–5
- Day 6: 2 Thessalonians 1–3
- Day 7: Catch up on any readings you've missed.

SEVERAL OF PAUL'S LETTERS were written while he was locked up. His body was confined, but his words traveled. And what did he keep talking about from behind those prison walls? Freedom. That paradox is the heart of discipleship: You can be bound and still free, pressed and still rejoicing, restricted yet unshaken in Christ.

To the Galatians, Paul proclaims, "It is for freedom that Christ has set us free" (Galatians 5:1). Yet in the same breath he adds, "Stand firm, then, and do not let yourselves be burdened again by a yoke of slavery." Freedom is not a slogan. It demands vigilance. It is not simply release from the past, but the daily commitment to live differently. Paul knows how easy it is to slip back into chains of fear, shame, or systems that strip us of dignity. Freedom is both gift and assignment.

That assignment always points us toward others. In Ephesians, Paul reminds us that freedom draws us into community. We are "one body" (Ephesians 2:16), each part bound to the other. Freedom is never an excuse to isolate or to hoard. It calls us to maturity, to use our gifts for the strengthening of the whole.

In Philippians, Paul shows what that looks like in practice. From a cell he writes, "For to me, to live is Christ and to die is gain" (Philippians 1:21). Joy radiates from him, not because his circumstances are easy, but because Christ's presence cannot be chained. Real freedom outlasts walls.

And when Paul writes to the Thessalonians, his message carries both tenderness and warning: "Encourage one another and build each other up" (1 Thessalonians 5:11). Yet he also cautions against idleness. Freedom without responsibility erodes into complacency. Freedom without commitment slips into chaos.

Sis, Paul's words are still true for us. The freedom we receive in Christ is not license to walk away from community or to believe we owe nothing to anyone. It makes us accountable in a new way—to God, to one another, and to the sacred community that sustains us.

That is why Paul's letters still breathe today. They remind us that true freedom is never selfish. It is communal. It is responsible. It is joy that sustains, endurance that strengthens, and faith that lasts.

You are free, but never free to forget your people. You are free, but also responsible for loving, serving, and enduring. This is the rhythm of discipleship: liberation tied to love, freedom yoked to responsibility.

SIT WITH IT

1. Where in your life have you been set free by Christ, but you still feel tempted to slip back into old chains?

2. How can you use your freedom not just for yourself, but to strengthen your community?

3. What responsibility comes with your freedom in this season, and how will you live it out with joy?

VERSE OF THE WEEK

It is for freedom that Christ has set us free. Stand firm, then, and do not let yourselves be burdened again by a yoke of slavery.

Galatians 5:1

WEEK 50
HOPE THAT HOLDS

DAILY READINGS

- Day 1: 1 Timothy 1–6
- Day 2: 2 Timothy 1–4
- Day 3: Titus 1–3
- Day 4: Philemon 1
- Day 5: 1 Peter 1–5
- Day 6: 2 Peter 1–3
- Day 7: Catch up on any readings you've missed.

HOW DOES FIRE REFINE hope? First, it strips away illusions. In suffering, the false promises we leaned on—status, money, control—fall away, leaving a hope anchored in God. Second, fire strengthens what is real. Just as gold grows purer when melted, trials reveal whether our hope is shallow or rooted. Third, fire teaches endurance. Hope that survives the blaze is no longer wishful thinking; it is disciplined trust. Finally, fire creates witness. Others can see refined hope shine when we rejoice through tears, keep showing up, or trust God even with scars.

Suffering, Peter explains, is not strange or unexpected. Hardship is not proof that God has abandoned us. Struggle is woven into what it means to belong to Christ. Trials may burn, but they also refine, like gold tested in fire.

In 1 Peter 4, Peter writes to believers scattered across the Roman Empire, under the shadow of persecution, during the early years of the church. They are ridiculed, pressured, and even hunted for following Christ. His words ring out with startling honesty: "Dear friends, do not be surprised at the fiery ordeal that has come on you to test you, as though something strange were happening to you" (1 Peter 4:12). Words meant to steady suffering believers.

But Peter does not stop at naming pain. In his second letter, he insists: "The Lord is not slow in keeping his promise, as some understand slowness. Instead he is patient with you" (2 Peter 3:9). Hope, for Peter, is not naive optimism. It is the steady trust that God's timing and presence outlast delay and despair.

We saw a glimpse of this kind of hope in 2022, during the confirmation hearings of Justice Ketanji Brown Jackson. She endured days of public scrutiny marked by hostility and thinly veiled bias. Many tried to diminish her worth or question her belonging, but she held her dignity with grace. She did not let the fire consume her; instead, her calm strength became witness to something deeper. And then came her historic appointment: the first Black woman seated on the United States Supreme Court. For those who had prayed and waited across generations, her confirmation was a living reminder that God is not slow in keeping promises. Delay is not denial. Hope refined by fire can become hope fulfilled.

Sis, we know this kind of hope. We have lived in the tension between fiery trial and unshakable faith. We've endured and kept showing up—for work, for worship, for our families, and for ourselves—with grief and joy hand in hand. Hope has held us when nothing else could.

Hope that holds is not soft. It is fire-tested, Spirit-breathed, and community-sustained. It is the witness that says: I may be pressed, but I am not crushed. *I may be refined, but I will not be consumed. And by God's grace, I will come forth as gold.*

SIT WITH IT

1. Where in your life do you feel the "fire" right now, and revealing what remains when illusions fall away? How might God be using it to refine your hope?

2. In a letter to Timothy, Paul urges him to guard the faith with "power, love, and self-discipline" (2 Timothy 1:7). "So do not be ashamed of the testimony about our Lord or of me his prisoner. Rather, join with me in suffering for the gospel, by the power of God" (2 Timothy 1:8). How does that encouragement strengthen your own discipleship when trials test you?

3. Who has shown you what fire-tested hope looks like, and how has their witness shaped your own faith?

THIS I PRAY

God of refining fire, thank You for meeting me in the heat of trial. When the flames rise, hold me steady in hope. Give me endurance when I want to give up, joy that defies despair, and patience to trust Your promises even when they seem delayed. May my life shine as a witness that hope is real, tested, and true. By Your grace, may I come forth as gold. In Jesus's name, amen.

WEEK 51
FAITH THAT KEEPS GOING

DAILY READINGS

- Day 1: Hebrews 1–7
- Day 2: Hebrews 8–13
- Day 3: James 1–5
- Day 4: 1 John 1–5
- Day 5: 2 John 1, 3 John 1
- Day 6: Jude 1
- Day 7: Catch up on any readings you've missed.

FAITH DOESN'T JUST NEED a spark; it needs staying power. These letters were not written for brand-new believers, but for disciples learning how to endure. Hebrews, James, and the shorter letters show us how to hold faith when the race feels long and the temptation to give up grows heavy.

Hebrews was written to a weary community tempted to drift away. Its writer paints vivid images of endurance: holding fast to confession, following the cloud of witnesses, and running with perseverance with eyes fixed on Jesus. James tells believers that trials are not punishment but formation: "The testing of your faith produces perseverance. Let perseverance finish its work so that you may be mature and complete" (James 1:3-4). Together, these voices remind us that discipleship is measured not by quick starts but by faithful endurance.

That truth lives in us as Black women. Perseverance isn't just an idea; it's also a way of life. Think of Althea Gibson, the first Black woman to break barriers in professional tennis. She faced racism and isolation, but she pressed forward. In her autobiography, *I Always Wanted to Be Somebody*, she wrote, "If I've made it, it's half because I was game to take a wicked amount of punishment along the way and half because there were an awful lot of people who cared enough to help me." Her story echoes Hebrews and James: Perseverance is forged in trial and sustained by faith and community.

Scripture also shows us how to endure. Hebrews urges us to hold on to hope and keep gathering for encouragement. James says faith grows when we practice it. John reminds us that to abide in Christ is to abide in love. Jude offers a blueprint: Build yourselves up in faith, pray in the Spirit, stay in God's love, and wait for His mercy.

Perseverance doesn't always feel holy. Sometimes it looks like exhaustion or crawling more than running. Yet the good news is that Jesus is not only the "pioneer" of our faith but also the "perfecter" (Hebrews 12:2). He ran this race first. He knows the weight of weariness and the sting of being misunderstood. When we stumble, Jesus does not shame us but strengthens us.

Sis, you don't have to sprint; you just have to stay in the race. Every step is a testimony. Every trial is shaping you into maturity. And when the finish line feels far, remember you are not running alone. Christ is with you, and a cloud of witnesses is already shouting your name. Keep going.

SIT WITH IT

1. How do Hebrews and James challenge you to see perseverance as more than endurance, but as growth in maturity?

2. Althea Gibson's perseverance made a way for others. How has someone else's endurance created a path for you—and how might yours make a way for others?

3. As you reflect on this year of Scripture, where can you celebrate your perseverance, however imperfect, as evidence of God's faithfulness in you?

BIBLE TRUTH

Hebrews 12 uses the image of a long-distance race to describe the life of faith. The chapter is written to believers who are weary, reminding them that faith is sustained not by speed but by enduring, and by keeping their eyes fixed on Jesus. The phrase "pioneer and perfecter of faith" (Hebrews 12:2) comes from the Greek words *archegos* (trailblazer) and *teleiotes* (finisher). Jesus is both the starting point and the sustaining strength of our faith—running before us, alongside us, and with us until the very end.

WEEK 52

FROM GARDEN TO GLORY

DAILY READINGS

- Day 1: Revelation 1–3
- Day 2: Revelation 4–7
- Day 3: Revelation 8–11
- Day 4: Revelation 12–15
- Day 5: Revelation 16–19
- Day 6: Revelation 20–22
- Day 7: Catch up on any readings you've missed.

WE'VE MADE IT TO the end of this yearlong journey, and to the final book of the Bible. Revelation is a letter, a prophecy, and a vision at once, full of strange images and powerful promises. Written to persecuted churches under Roman government, its purpose was never to terrify but to encourage: to remind weary disciples that the government does not have the last word. God does.

To read Revelation faithfully is to see it as a survival text, assuring struggling believers their suffering is not the end. That makes it deeply relevant for us as Black women. We know what it is to live in survival mode and we have held faith when everything says to give up. Revelation offers a different future: "He will wipe every tear from their eyes. There will be no more death or mourning or crying or pain, for the old order of things has passed away" (Revelation 21:4).

The Bible begins in a garden (Genesis 2), where sin fractures Creation and exile follows. Yet in Revelation 22, the garden reappears inside the holy city. A river of life flows clear as crystal, and the tree of life stands tall, "bearing twelve crops of fruit, yielding its fruit every month. And the leaves of the tree are for the healing of the nations" (Revelation 22:2). Twelve crops signal unending abundance for God's people. The healing leaves promise restoration for every wound and every nation. For us, this ought to be more than metaphor. That's good news. What was lost in the garden is restored in glory. The circle is complete: Creation renewed, fellowship restored, life everlasting.

Revelation also promises every injustice endured, every sorrow carried, every weary mile walked will not be wasted. The Lamb who was slain is also the One who reigns. So every believer who overcomes can trust the promise: "I will give the right to eat from the tree of life" (Revelation 2:7).

Sis, we've come this far by faith. Not perfect faith, but persevering faith. Celebrate God's work and be proud of how much we've grown. Every prayer, every page, every moment of trust is a testament to grace and endurance. Glory belongs to God, yet your steady "yes" matters too.

Just as Genesis opens with God's breath giving life, Revelation closes with God's voice saying, "Yes, I am coming soon" (Revelation 22:20). Our story ends not in despair, but in promise. Hold fast, overcome, and know this: Your faith will carry you all the way from the garden to the glory.

SIT WITH IT

1. How does Revelation's closing vision of healing and restoration shape your hope for your own life and for the world?

2. What does it mean to you that the tree of life bears so much fruit and its leaves are for the healing of the nations?

3. Looking back over this year's journey through Scripture, what growth, insights, or transformations are you most grateful for?

THIS I PRAY

God of beginnings and endings, thank You for walking with me through this year in Your Word. From the first pages of Genesis to the final vision of Revelation, You have shown Yourself as Creator, Redeemer, Sustainer, and Friend. Thank You for every promise that steadied me, every challenge that stretched me, and every word that gave me life.

As I finish this journey, I pause to celebrate Your faithfulness and to honor the growth You have brought forth in me. My steps have not been perfect, but You have made them purposeful. My faith has not been flawless, but it has been formed. Where I felt weary, You carried me. Where I felt uncertain, You spoke peace. Where I doubted, You reminded me of Your love.

Now, as Revelation promises, I trust that one day every tear will be wiped away, every injustice overturned, and every ache redeemed. Until that day, let me live as one who overcomes—rooted in Your Word, held by Your Spirit, and strengthened by sacred community.

From the garden to the glory, You are God, and I am Yours. Amen.

GROUP STUDY GUIDE

1. Go around the room and allow each person to share their favorite chapter or verse from the week's readings.
2. How do you interpret this particular text? What do you hear the author saying?
3. Are there any companion scriptures that you know will complement this text?
4. As you read the text, do you see more of God's love, God's mercy, or God's justice? Explain.
5. How can this text be applied to your life?
6. Can you identify with any particular character within the text? Can you see yourself in this text in any way?
7. After reading the weekly commentary, what will you do differently as you go forward?
8. How have this week's readings encouraged you to do better and be better?
9. After reading the Scripture and commentary, what principles have you acquired that you might teach others?
10. Take a moment to encourage the person sitting next to you based upon something you have read in the text.

RESOURCES

The journey doesn't end here. If this devotional has stirred questions, healed wounds, or opened new doors of curiosity, you'll find companions in the resources given here. I've chosen them with Black women in mind—voices that honor our stories, challenge our faith, and invite us deeper into God's Word. Some are tools for daily study, others are classics of womanist thought, and still others are testimonies of preaching and survival. Take your time. Pick up what speaks to you in this season. Let these resources carry you further on the path.

WEBSITE

BibleProject.com offers short, engaging videos that explain books and themes of Scripture, weaving together art, theology, and accessibility.

BOOKS

Daughters of Thunder: Black Women Preachers and Their Sermons, 1850–1979
Edited by Bettye Collier-Thomas
A historic collection of sermons amplifying the voices of Black women who shaped the pulpit long before recognition.

I Found God in Me: A Womanist Biblical Hermeneutics Reader
Edited by Mitzi J. Smith
Essays that highlight Black women's voices and methods in biblical interpretation, offering fresh and liberating perspectives.

Jesus and the Disinherited
By Howard Thurman
A timeless classic showing how Jesus speaks directly to the oppressed, offering courage, dignity, and spiritual resistance.

Just a Sister Away: Understanding the Timeless Connection Between Women of Today and Women in the Bible
By Renita J. Weems
A groundbreaking reflection on biblical women's stories, exploring friendship, betrayal, and healing through a womanist lens of faith.

Sisters in the Wilderness: The Challenge of Womanist God-Talk
By Delores S. Williams
A classic in womanist theology, reflecting on Hagar's story and survival as sacred.

Stony the Road We Trod: African American Biblical Interpretation
Edited by Cain Hope Felder
A pioneering collection of African American biblical interpretation, amplifying Black voices and perspectives in Scripture study.

True to Our Native Land: An African American New Testament Commentary
Edited by Brian K. Blount, Gay L. Byron, and Emerson B. Powery
The first African American New Testament commentary, bringing scholarship and Black faith experience together for powerful insights.

Walking Through the Valley: Womanist Explorations in the Spirit of Katie Geneva Cannon
Edited by Emilie Townes, Stacey Floyd-Thomas, Alison P. Gise Johnson, and Angela Sims
Essays honoring Katie Geneva Cannon's legacy, expanding womanist ethics, theology, and spirituality for today.

Womanist Midrash: A Reintroduction to the Women of the Torah and the Throne
By Wilda C. Gafney
A groundbreaking rereading of women in Hebrew Scripture, centering their stories with depth, dignity, and womanist imagination.

REFERENCES

American Association of University Women (AAUW). "The Simple Truth About the Gender Pay Gap." 2022. https://www.aauw.org/resources/research/simple-truth/.

Collier-Thomas, Bettye. *Daughters of Thunder: Black Women Preachers and Their Sermons, 1850–1979*. Jossey-Bass Publishers, 1997.

Epstein, Rebecca, Jamilia J. Blake, and Thalia González. "Girlhood Interrupted: The Erasure of Black Girls' Childhood." Georgetown Law Center on Poverty and Inequality. 2017. https://www.law.georgetown.edu/poverty-inequality-center/wp-content/uploads/sites/14/2017/08/girlhood-interrupted.pdf.

Gibson, Althea. *I Always Wanted to Be Somebody*. New Chapter Press, 2013.

National Women's Law Center. "Black Women and the Wage Gap." 2022. https://nwlc.org/resource/wage-gap-black-women/.

Turner, Steve. *Amazing Grace: The Story of America's Most Beloved Song*. HarperOne, 2002.

INDEX

K

L

M